Disc

TUDOR
LONDON

A Journey Back in Time

Natalie Grueninger

The
History
Press

I dedicate this book to my beloved children,
Isabel and Tristan.

First published 2017

The History Press
The Mill, Brimscombe Port
Stroud, Gloucestershire, GL5 2QG
www.thehistorypress.co.uk
© Natalie Grueninger, 2017

The right of Natalie Grueninger to be identified as the Author
of this work has been asserted in accordance with the
Copyright, Designs and Patents Act 1988.

British Library Cataloguing in Publication Data.
A catalogue record for this book is available from the British Library.

ISBN 978 0 7509 7015 0

Typesetting and origination by The History Press
Printed in Turkey by Imak

CONTENTS

ACKNOWLEDGEMENTS

My sincerest thanks to Mark Beynon and the staff at The History Press for making this book possible. Thank you to my sister, Karina, for taking the time to read and offer feedback on my writing, and for the many laughs, inspiring conversations and flutes of champers along the way. Gratitude also to my mother, one of the most talented writers I've ever known, for instilling in me a love of words. My sincere thanks also go to the curators and co-ordinators who so graciously corresponded with me over email, answering my many questions and assisting me to acquire some of the wonderful images presented in this book. A special thanks to my dear friend Sarah Morris, for welcoming me into her home on my last research trip, and also to Val, for taking the time to show me around Tudor Hackney. A special thanks to the visitors to my website (www.onthetudortrail.com) and the online Tudor community on Facebook, Twitter and Instagram for their enthusiastic contributions, friendship and continued support. And most importantly, I would like to offer a heartfelt thanks to my husband and children, Chris, Isabel and Tristan, without whom this book could not have been written. Thank you for your constant support, love and encouragement, and for understanding and respecting my love of sixteenth-century England.

Let no one say the past is dead.
The past is all about us and within.

Oodgeroo Noonuccal

INTRODUCTION

The past has always called to me. For as long as I can remember, I have been attuned to the velvety whispers of those who have walked this earth before me, silvery fingers beckoning me to follow, compelling me to journey back in time to discover more about the people and events, now seemingly lost to us. For the last seven years I've pursued these voices, and dedicated many hours and much energy to researching and writing about the Tudors, through the lens of the great houses, palaces and castles where their stories unfurled.

This love of learning history on the very stage where it played out led me to create, in 2009, 'On the Tudor Trail', a website dedicated to documenting historic sites associated with Anne Boleyn and sharing information about prominent Tudor personalities and daily life in sixteenth-century England. In 2013, my debut book, *In the Footsteps of Anne Boleyn*, co-authored with Sarah Morris, was published in the UK, followed by *In the Footsteps of the Six Wives of Henry VIII*, another collaboration between Sarah and myself, in March 2016.

Why the fascination with places? These sites are the keepers of history, the guardians of stories, whose protagonists have long returned to dust. They are portals between our world and theirs.

Through reading, we can come to know the Tudors, intellectually. We can learn about the larger-than-life personalities, the politics and great personal dramas that so captivate us, and spend hours poring over their personal correspondence, state papers and portraits. But when we stand where the Tudors once stood and see what they saw, our connection deepens. Suddenly, they step out from the pages of history books and become living, breathing people once more.

It's in these moments that things I've read about and thought I had understood finally hit home, bringing fresh insights. It's also when I experience the strongest emotional connection to the past, which is precisely wherein lies the power of places – in their ability to touch us emotionally, to leap the chasm between past and present and unite us on a soul level.

When I stand in a place – be it an intact building, ruins or even an empty field – that once bore witness to the defining moments of the era, and the quiet ones too, and absorb its history and its moods, I feel that great gulf close and time gradually dissipate. In those moments, the past feels as though it's standing alongside me.

Tyburn Tree (Gallows) Plaque, 2016. This plaque, found on the traffic island at the junction of Bayswater and Edgeware Roads, marks the approximate location of the notorious Tyburn gallows, where thousands of people lost their lives. (Author's collection)

THE BIRTH OF DISCOVERING TUDOR LONDON

This project was inspired by the many people who've contacted me over the years, asking for suggestions of places to visit in London, associated with the Tudors. Often people are only visiting London for a long weekend, and so are eager to discover what the 'must-see' places are. Frequently, I'm asked to suggest longer itineraries, such as five, seven or ten-day trips, and am regularly asked for suggestions of places to visit that are off the main tourist trail. While I responded to each request individually, an idea was sparked, and I felt compelled to write a guidebook to sites associated with the Tudors in London, which could all be comfortably visited in a ten-day stay.

The challenging part was selecting which places to include. In the end I chose to feature both buildings associated with or built by the Tudors, and the galleries and museums that house treasures from this period of history. Because just as places can transport us back in time and connect us to people and events from long ago, so too can *things*. They can be powerful conduits of moments. For example, a handwritten letter to a lover recalls a very specific point in time, and allows us to share in a potent heart-felt experience.

I also decided to include only those places where there is something substantial left to see, and importantly, which are open to the public. This immediately ruled out some major sites, such as that of Tyburn Gallows, Greenwich Palace and Whitehall Palace, all of which played an important role in the story of the Tudors, but where, sadly, there is nothing or very little left to see above ground. It also meant excluding places like St James' Palace and Crosby Hall, as they are not open to the public.

Hence, this book is not a comprehensive guide but rather a curated guide to what I consider the best of Tudor London, based on the above principles.

The Old Royal Naval College, Greenwich, 2013. Beneath the Old Royal Naval College in Greenwich lie the remains of Greenwich Palace, a favoured Tudor residence, where Henry VIII, Mary I and Elizabeth I were born. (Author's collection)

HOW TO USE THIS BOOK

In Part 1 of *Discovering Tudor London*, you'll find four suggested itineraries of varying lengths, covering sites in London and Greater London. The one exception to this rule is the inclusion of Hampton Court Palace in Surrey, an exceptional Tudor time capsule. More survives of Hampton Court than any other Tudor palace, and so I felt compelled to include it in this guidebook. Next to each location in Part 1 you'll find a page number, which corresponds to the entry for that location in the book. Here you'll find information about the location, including a short history; a description, if known, of the building's appearance in the sixteenth century; a summary of the key events that took place there and a visitor information section. The individual entries will also provide you with contact details, tips on where to eat, what to see, nearest tube station etc. A map to help you gauge distances also accompanies the itineraries.

Of course, rather than follow my suggested itineraries, you can organise your own but do keep in mind that certain locations are only open on certain days, and so be sure to check opening hours carefully to avoid being disappointed. If you're visiting some of the smaller churches, I suggest you email ahead to confirm visiting hours, as these often close with little or no notice.

The thirty-two main locations included in this guidebook are organised into the following three sections: Part 2: Houses, Halls, Palaces & Castles, Part 3: Churches & Religious Houses and Part 4: Museums & Galleries. An extensive range of illustrations, including photographs and paintings, complements the text.

My sincerest hope is that this book will help bring London's Tudor past to life, and make the task of planning your own Tudor London pilgrimage much easier.

I do hope you enjoy your journey back in time!

Natalie Grueninger
2016

A TASTE OF TUDOR LONDON

At the beginning of the sixteenth century, Tudor London was a bustling city of around 60,000 inhabitants. The City came under the jurisdiction of the lord mayor and sheriffs of London, whose job it was to maintain order and cleanliness. It was the most prosperous city in England, on account of it being a flourishing trading centre and an important port, and was by far the largest city in the country, rapidly becoming one of the biggest in Europe. To offer some comparison, the second largest city in Tudor England was Norwich, which at the beginning of the Tudor reign had a population of about 10,600.

London (or Londinium) was founded in Roman times, in around AD 50, although most historians agree that the region had been occupied for thousands of years before then.

In about AD 200 the Romans built a defensive wall and ditch around the city to protect its inhabitants from attack and to make the job of collecting taxes easier. These walls, around 6m high, remained long after the Roman occupation ended and defined the boundaries of Tudor London. However, by the sixteenth century, the city's population had already begun to spill out beyond these limits, and two smaller towns lay outside the walled city, Southwark, on the south bank of the Thames, and Westminster – the seat of government.

The ancient Roman walls enclosed a space of around 1 square mile, and were bounded by open fields to the north and the Thames to the south. In this relatively small area there were around 100 parishes, each comprising only of a few streets. Apart from the 100 plus parish churches, there was also the great cathedral of St Paul and a number of religious houses. The London skyline was dominated by spires and towers,

the tallest of which was the steeple of St Paul, which rose to around 460ft, until it was destroyed in 1561 after being struck by lightning. Just outside the city walls, to the east, stood the Tower of London, as it still does to this day.

Immediately beyond the wall was the ditch, a constant cause of headache for the authorities, who despite their best efforts were unable to dissuade people from using it as a sewer and dumping ground. One can just imagine the smell that emanated from there!

The city wall, which had over the years been rebuilt and repaired, extended from Tower Hill in the east to Blackfriars in the west, and was punctuated by seven main gates – Aldgate, Bishopsgate, Moorgate (built in 1415), Cripplegate, Aldersgate, Newgate and Ludgate. These were not gates in the modern sense, but rather multi-storey buildings that contained an archway or two for traffic to pass through and were protected by a portcullis and other defensive features. They often served as accommodation – in the case of Cripplegate, Aldersgate, Ludgate and Newgate, as prisons too – but perhaps their most grisly function was as a place to display the dismembered body parts of traitors. In June 1497, the leaders of the Cornish Rebellion were hung, drawn and quartered at Tyburn, about a 3-mile walk west of the city, and some of their limbs nailed to the city gates. There was also a gate at the southern end of London Bridge, where the severed heads of traitors were

A nineteenth-century reconstruction of the City of London and its environs in Tudor times by H.W. Brewer. Old St Paul's Cathedral is visible in the background, and in the foreground, a section of the Tower of London's moat and the scaffold on Tower Hill. (Author's collection)

regularly displayed, the first of which is recorded as having been that of William Wallace, executed in 1305.

After curfew, rung by the bells of St Mary-le-Bow and other churches at around 9 p.m. in summer or dusk in winter, the gates were locked for the night, and not reopened until dawn. During this time, no one was permitted entry into the City and those inside the walls had to leave the streets and return to their homes – undoubtedly the safest place to be, at least after dark. The narrow and crowded streets of Tudor London could be very dangerous. The threat of meeting some unsavoury character was a very real possibility but it was not your only concern.

Apart from the principal streets, most were unpaved and their surfaces uneven. At times they were made almost impassable by ruts and holes. Those streets that were cobbled were often slippery and muddy, and difficult to navigate, especially at night. It's little wonder that Londoners only ventured out after curfew in exceptional circumstances.

As for cleanliness, in theory each citizen was required to keep the space in front of his or her house relatively clean, whether this was strictly adhered to is uncertain. Like today, there would have been householders that took extra pride in the appearance of their street frontage, and others who did not. While some of the larger houses had enclosed latrines that emptied into deep cesspits, most would have made do with a bucket or 'close stool', which would be emptied daily into a stream or river, or into the ditch surrounding the city.

The twisting lanes and alleys were dark even on the brightest day, because Tudor homes were often built with the first floor overhanging the street, so close in fact that from your first floor window you could almost touch your neighbour across the street.

Apart from being gloomy and very likely smelly, the streets were also very noisy. Church bells dictated the day's activities, market bells rang to mark the beginning and end of trading, tradesmen and pedlars shouted about their wares to passers-by, animals – namely pigs – roamed freely and the town criers delivered the latest news. Probably noisiest of all, were the metalworkers, including the blacksmiths, farriers and cutlers whose clanging and hammering could be heard from a distance. A walk around Tudor London would have been an assault on the senses.

The City was also a place of contrasts. While many of the alleys were narrow and lined with humble houses, where the poor of London lived, other streets were wide and bordered by grand four- and five-storey residences that boasted glass in all their windows – homes to the city's rich merchant population. Cheapside was one such street. It was the widest street in Tudor London, the principal market place and home to several conduits, including the Great Conduit, a large stone fountain where each day, people lined up to collect water. It was also an important part of the ancient coronation route from the Tower of London to Westminster.

The congested streets and insalubrious back alleys, meant that, whenever possible, Londoners preferred to travel by water. The main thoroughfare and the heart of the city was the Thames. There, Londoners or visitors could hire a wherry to take them up and down the river, where at any one time there could be hundreds of boats, ranging from small vessels to dung-boats and merchant ships on the water. About twenty or so quays and wharves lined the north bank of the river from the Tower up to London Bridge.

In the sixteenth century, this ancient monument was considered one of the great wonders of the world. It was completed in 1209 and, until the eighteenth century, was the only bridge to traverse the Thames in London. The bridge was supported by twenty Gothic arches, built on piers and protected by vast timber starlings, which significantly narrowed the water channels, and led to a torrent of water pouring between them at high and low tides. To venture under the bridge at these times was extremely dangerous, and known as 'shooting the bridge'.

The road that ran along the length of the bridge was around 275m long and 6m wide at its widest, although in some

Temple Bar, 2016. This was the principal ceremonial entrance to the City of London from Westminster. It once stood on the junction of Fleet Street and the Strand. This monument, designed by Sir Christopher Wren, is the successor to the medieval gate, which stood in Tudor times. (Author's collection)

A reconstruction of Tudor Cheapside by H.W. Brewer. Old St Paul's Cathedral can be seen in the background, St Mary-le-Bow on the left and the great conduit in the centre. (Author's collection)

19

sections it narrowed to less than 4m, just one lane north and one south, shared by pedestrians, carts and horses.

This reduction in space was a result of the buildings that crowded the bridge and ran almost its entire length, including houses and shops – the rent from which paid for the upkeep of the bridge – public toilets, a chapel and a drawbridge. These buildings projected out over the river and were often joined across the roadway, transforming the bridge into a tunnel in places.

The medieval bridge stood until 1831, by which time a new bridge, designed by John Rennie, had been built about 55m west of the old bridge, which was then dismantled. Rennie's bridge, however, did not survive as long as its predecessor and

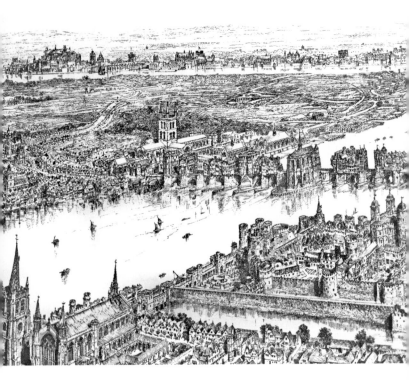

by 1973 a new bridge had been erected on the same site – the present-day London Bridge.

By the end of the Tudor reign, the population of London is estimated to have quadrupled and risen to somewhere in the vicinity of 200,000. As a result of the serious overcrowding and poor public sanitation, Tudor Londoners suffered from many diseases, including smallpox, measles, malaria, typhus and dysentery. Outbreaks of the 'sweating sickness' also occurred throughout this period. This highly contagious and often fatal disease could kill a person within hours of the first symptom. In 1551, it claimed the lives of both teenage sons of Charles Brandon and Catherine Willoughby, within hours of each other.

As the hub of trade and industry, and the centre of literature and the arts, London continued to draw people from all over the country and abroad. At the close of the sixteenth century, as the sun began to set on the Tudor reign, the historian John Stow described it as the 'fairest, largest, richest and best inhabited city in the world'.

This diverse and vibrant city, however, would suffer greatly over the succeeding centuries, when fire and war would

A nineteenth-century reconstruction of the City of London and its environs in Tudor times by H.W. Brewer. In the top left corner stands Westminster Palace, next to which can be seen Whitehall Palace. In the centre is Old London Bridge, and in the foreground, the Tower of London. In the bottom left-hand corner is St Katherine's. (Author's collection)

A nineteenth-century reconstruction of the City of London and its environs
in Tudor times by H.W. Brewer. In the background, from left to right, are
St Bartholomew the Great, the Charterhouse, St John's Clerkenwell and
St James' Priory Clerkenwell. (Author's collection)

destroy much of its ancient fabric. Some buildings, though,
remarkably survived, and stand today as a testament to the
short-lived but captivating Tudor dynasty.

TUDOR TIMELINE

1485
22 August ∾ Henry Tudor defeats Richard III at the Battle of Bosworth and becomes the first king of the House of Tudor

1486
18 January ∾ Henry VII marries Elizabeth of York, uniting the Houses of Lancaster and York

1491
28 June ∾ Prince Henry Tudor (later Henry VIII) is born

1501
14 November ∾ Prince Arthur marries Katherine of Aragon at old St Paul's Cathedral

1502
2 April ∾ Prince Arthur dies at Ludlow Castle

1503
11 February ∾ Elizabeth of York dies at the Tower of London

8 August ∾ Princess Margaret marries James IV of Scotland

1509
21 April ∾ Death of Henry VII and accession of Henry VIII

11 June ∿ Henry VIII marries Katherine of Aragon, his brother's widow

24 June ∿ Henry VIII and Katherine of Aragon are crowned at Westminster Abbey

29 June ∿ Death of Margaret Beaufort, mother of Henry VII and grandmother of Henry VIII

1514
15 September ∿ Thomas Wolsey appointed Archbishop of York

9 October ∿ Princess Mary Tudor marries Louis XII of France

1515
February ∿ After the death of Louis XII, Princess Mary secretly marries Charles Brandon, Duke of Suffolk

September ∿ Thomas Wolsey appointed cardinal

1516
18 February ∿ Princess Mary Tudor (later Mary I) is born

1519
15 June ∿ Birth of Henry Fitzroy, illegitimate son of Henry VIII by Elizabeth Blount

1520
7–24 June ∿ Field of the Cloth of Gold

1529
25 October ∿ Sir Thomas More appointed Lord Chancellor

1530
29 November ∾ Thomas Wolsey dies at Leicester Abbey

1532
1 September ∾ Anne Boleyn is made Marquess of Pembroke

16 May ∾ Sir Thomas More resigns as Lord Chancellor

11 October ∾ Henry VIII and Anne Boleyn sail to Calais to meet Francis I

1533
25 January ∾ Henry VIII marries Anne Boleyn

30 March ∾ Thomas Cranmer is consecrated as Archbishop of Canterbury

1 June ∾ Anne Boleyn is crowned at Westminster Abbey

25 June ∾ Mary Tudor, former queen of France and sister of Henry VIII, dies at Westhorpe Hall in Suffolk

11 July ∾ Pope Clement VII excommunicates King Henry VIII

7 September ∾ Princess Elizabeth (later Elizabeth I) is born at Greenwich Palace

1534
April ∾ Thomas Cromwell is appointed the king's principal secretary

1535
6 July ∾ Sir Thomas More is executed

1536

7 January ∾ Katherine of Aragon dies

17 May ∾ George Boleyn, Henry Norris, Francis Weston, William Brereton and Mark Smeaton are executed on Tower Hill

19 May ∾ Anne Boleyn is executed at the Tower of London

30 May ∾ Henry VIII marries Jane Seymour

22 (or 23) July ∾ Henry Fitzroy, Duke of Richmond, dies at St James' Palace

October–December ∾ Pilgrimage of Grace

1537

12 October ∾ Prince Edward (later Edward VI) is born at Hampton Court Palace

24 October ∾ Queen Jane Seymour dies at Hampton Court Palace

1538

17 December ∾ Pope Paul III excommunicates King Henry VIII

1540

6 January ∾ Henry VIII marries Anne of Cleves

9 July ∾ Henry VIII's marriage to Anne of Cleves is declared null and void

28 July ∾ Thomas Cromwell is executed at the Tower of London

28 July ∾ Henry VIII marries Catherine Howard

1541

18 October ∾ Death of Margaret Tudor, sister of Henry VIII

10 December ∾ Thomas Culpeper and Francis Dereham, alleged lovers of Catherine Howard, are executed for treason at Tyburn

1542
13 February ∾ Catherine Howard and Jane Boleyn are executed at the Tower of London

14 December ∾ Death of James V of Scotland, Accession of Mary, Queen of Scots

1543
12 July ∾ Henry VIII marries Katherine Parr at Hampton Court Palace

1545
19 July ∾ The *Mary Rose* sinks

1546
16 July ∾ Anne Askew burnt at the stake at Smithfield, alongside John Lascelles

1547
28 January ∾ Death of Henry VIII and accession of Edward VI

20 February ∾ Edward VI is crowned at Westminster Abbey

June ∾ Katherine Parr's marriage to Thomas Seymour becomes public knowledge

1548
30 August ∾ Katherine Parr gives birth to a daughter at Sudeley Castle

5 September ∾ Katherine Parr dies at Sudeley Castle

1553

6 July ∽ Edward VI dies at Greenwich Palace

10 July ∽ Lady Jane Grey is proclaimed queen

1 October ∽ Queen Mary I is crowned at Westminster Abbey

1554

12 February ∽ Lady Jane Grey and her husband, Guildford Dudley are executed at the Tower of London

18 March ∽ Princess Elizabeth is imprisoned in the Tower of London following Wyatt's rebellion, and later put under house arrest at the palace at Woodstock

25 July ∽ Queen Mary marries Philip of Spain at Winchester Cathedral

1555

April ∽ Princess Elizabeth returns to court

October ∽ Queen Mary gives permission for her half-sister, Elizabeth, to return to her house at Hatfield

1556

21 March ∽ Thomas Cranmer is burnt at the stake

1557

16 July ∽ Anne of Cleves dies at Chelsea Manor

1558

7 January ∽ Calais falls to the French

17 November ∽ Death of Queen Mary and accession of Elizabeth I

1559

15 January ∾ Elizabeth I is crowned at Westminster Abbey

1564

26 April ∾ William Shakespeare is baptised at the Holy Trinity Parish Church in Stratford

1566

19 June ∾ Mary, Queen of Scots gives birth to Prince James of Scotland (later James I of England)

1580

26 September ∾ Sir Francis Drake returns to England aboard the *Golden Hinde*, after having circumnavigated the globe

1587

8 February ∾ Mary, Queen of Scots is executed at Fotheringhay Castle

1588

July–August ∾ The Spanish Armada

4 September ∾ Robert Dudley, Earl of Leicester, dies

1603

24 March ∾ Death of Elizabeth I and accession of James I

Part 1

Map &

Suggested

Itineraries

Discovering Tudor London

1. Hampton Court Palace (Surrey)
2. The National Archives
3. Fulham Palace
4. Victoria and Albert Museum
5. Chelsea Old Church
6. Tate Britain
7. The British Library
8. Sutton House
9. Eltham Palace and Gardens
10. The Jewel Tower
11. Westminster Abbey

River Thames

12. Westminster Hall
13. St Margaret's Church
14. National Portrait Gallery
15. The British Museum
16. The Garden Museum
17. Lambeth Palace
18. Lincoln's Inn
19. St Dunstan-in-the-West
20. St Etheldreda's Church
21. Museum of the Order of St John
22. The Charterhouse
23. St Bartholomew the Great
24. Museum of London
25. Christchurch Greyfriars Church Garden
26. Guildhall
27. St Helen's, Bishopsgate
28. St Olave, Hart Street
29. St Magnus the Martyr
30. All Hallows by the Tower
31. The Tower of London
32. Southwark Cathedral

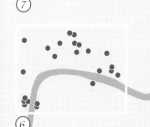

River Thames

London City Detail

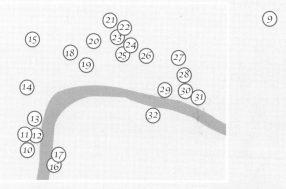

This map is for illustrative purposes only and designed to show the approximate location of each of the historic sites featured in this book.

3 DAYS

Friday

Full day at Hampton Court Palace (Page 66)
Evening visit to the Victoria and Albert Museum
(Page 240)

Saturday

Jewel Tower (Page 83)
Westminster Abbey (Page 206)
St Margaret's Church (Page 192)
National Portrait Gallery (Page 225)

Sunday

All Hallows by the Tower (Page 145)
Tower of London/Tower Hill (Page 115)
Southwark Cathedral (Page 157)

5 DAYS

Monday

Hampton Court Palace (Page 66)

Tuesday

Eltham Palace & Gardens (Page 44)
Victoria and Albert Museum (Page 240)

Wednesday

All Hallows by the Tower (Page 145)
Tower of London/Tower Hill (Page 115)
St Magnus the Martyr (Page 187)
Southwark Cathedral (Page 157)

Thursday

Guildhall (Page 60)
Sutton House (Page 109)
The British Library (Page 231)

Friday

Jewel Tower (Page 83)
Westminster Abbey (Page 206)
St Margaret's Church (Page 192)
National Portrait Gallery (Page 225)
The British Museum (Page 215)

7 DAYS

Monday

Eltham Palace & Gardens (Page 44)
Victoria and Albert Museum (Page 240)

Tuesday

All Hallows by the Tower (Page 145)
Tower of London/Tower Hill (Page 115)
St Magnus the Martyr (Page 187)
Southwark Cathedral (Page 157)

Wednesday

Guided tour of Lambeth Palace (Page 93)
The Garden Museum (Page 233)
Tate Britain (Page 229)

Thursday

Guildhall (Page 60)
Sutton House (Page 109)
The British Library (Page 231)

Friday

Jewel Tower (Page 83)
Westminster Abbey (Page 206)
St Margaret's Church (Page 192)

National Portrait Gallery (Page 225)
The British Museum (Page 215)

Saturday

Guided tour of the Museum of the Order of St John (Page 220)
Guided tour of the Charterhouse (Page 199)
Museum of London (Page 217)

Sunday

Hampton Court Palace (Page 66)

10 DAYS

Monday

Eltham Palace & Gardens (Page 44)
Victoria and Albert Museum (Page 240)

Tuesday

All Hallows by the Tower (Page 145)
Tower of London/Tower Hill (Page 115)
St Magnus the Martyr (Page 187)
Southwark Cathedral (Page 157)

Wednesday

Guided tour of Lambeth Palace (Page 93)
The Garden Museum (Page 233)
Tate Britain (Page 229)

Thursday

Guildhall (Page 60)
Sutton House (Page 109)
The British Library (Page 231)

Friday

Jewel Tower (Page 83)
Westminster Abbey (Page 206)

St Margaret's Church (Page 192)
National Portrait Gallery (Page 225)

Saturday

Guided tour of the Museum of the Order of St John (Page 220)
Guided tour of the Charterhouse (Page 199)
Museum of London (Page 217)

Sunday

Hampton Court Palace (Page 66)

Monday

The National Archives (Page 238)
Fulham Palace (Page 52)
Chelsea Old Church (Page 149)

Tuesday

A walk around the precincts of Lincoln's Inn
– guided tours are on hold until January 2018
(Page 101)
London Church's Walk – St Dunstan-in-
the-West (Page 172), St Etheldreda's (Page
177), St Bartholomew the Great (Page 165),
Christchurch Greyfriars Church Garden (Page
154), St Helen's, Bishopsgate (Page 183) and St
Olave's (Page 196)

Wednesday

Guided tour of the Houses of Parliament, only
available on weekdays during parliamentary
recesses (Page 132)
The British Museum (Page 215)

MUST-HAVES FOR A TUDOR LONDON PILGRIMAGE

- An Oyster Card (London travel card) – buy your card before you leave home and it will be delivered to your home address. (I used approximately £60 of credit for my ten-day stay in London.) For more information, visit: www.tfl.gov.uk/travel-information/visiting-london/visitor-oyster-card

- Your Historic Royal Palaces card (for more information, see the *Visitor Information* section at the end of the Tower of London entry)

- London Underground (Tube) map, available to download from VisitLondon.com

- Central London Tourist Map. A map of the city churches is also handy, download one from the Friends of the City Churches: www.london-city-churches.org.uk/PDFs/FCC_churches_map_web.pdf

- Comfortable walking shoes

- Waterproof/windproof jacket that fits in your day bag

- Small umbrella that fits in your day bag

- Spare change to purchase guidebooks/postcards from the churches you visit

- A camera of course!

Part 2

Houses, Halls, Palaces & Castles

I was staying at Lord Mountjoy's country house, when Thomas More came to see me, and took me out with him for a walk as far as the next village [Eltham], where all the king's children, except Prince Arthur, who was then the eldest son were being educated.

Erasmus recalled a visit to Eltham Palace in the autumn of 1499.

By the fourteenth century, Eltham Palace was one of the grandest and most favoured royal residences in England. Among its long list of distinguished royal visitors are Henry VI, Margaret of Anjou, Edward IV, Henry VII, and all subsequent Tudor monarchs. Its history can be traced back to at least 1086, when it's recorded in the Domesday Book as belonging to William the Conqueror's half-brother, Odo, Earl of Kent and bishop of Bayeux. Odo lost possession of Eltham in 1088, and the next 200 years witnessed several changes in ownership, until Bishop Antony Bek acquired the manor in 1295.

Bek appears to have rebuilt the manor house and constructed a defensive wall inside the line of the moat, punctuated by a number of octagonal bastions. He also created a hunting park, which would become very popular with the country's elite. The house was luxurious enough to host royalty, with Edward I and his son, the future Edward II, being regular guests of the bishop, who in 1305 gifted the manor to the Prince of Wales. This marked the beginning of Eltham's royal ownership.

The Great Hall at Eltham Palace, as it may have appeared in c. 1365. Illustration by G.F. Sargent, engraved by J. Godfrey. (Copyright Sarah Morris)

The Tudor Years

Successive monarchs enlarged and beautified the buildings and grounds, lavishing large sums of money on the palace. In the 1470s, Edward IV built the magnificent, surviving Great Hall that in 1482 was the setting for a Christmas feast for some 2,000 guests. He also enlarged two of the existing hunting parks, and created an additional one.

During the reign of Henry VII, Eltham served as a royal nursery where the future Henry VIII was raised and educated, alongside his sisters Margaret and Mary. It is uncertain as to whether the first of the Tudor monarchs made any significant additions or alterations to the palace complex, however, his son and successor certainly did, including the building of new privy apartments for himself, alterations to the queen's lodgings, and a tiltyard to the east of the palace. The most notable of the works commissioned by Henry VIII, however, was the rebuilding of the chapel in the inner courtyard, which when completed, rivalled Edward IV's Great Hall in size and splendour.

During the 1520s, Eltham was one of only six 'greater houses' large enough to accommodate the entire court with ease. Despite this, during the 1530s, the court visited only rarely, and Eltham continued to function primarily as a royal nursery. The king's attention and favour had moved further westwards, to Whitehall and Hampton Court Palace, and furthermore, the perennial Tudor favourite, Greenwich Palace, lay just 2 miles to the north-west. In the *Perambulation of Kent*, first published in 1576, the author, William Lambarde, observes:

> ... this house [Eltham] by reason of the nearnesse to Greenwiche ... hath not bene so greatly esteemed: the rather also for that the pleasures of the embarked groundes here, may be in manner as well enjoyed, the court lying at Greenwich, as if it were at this house it selfe.

Edward VI and Mary I maintained and repaired the palace, as did Elizabeth I, who, despite only visiting occasionally, commissioned some important works.

The Palace in its Heyday

Two surviving surveys of Eltham Palace made by the surveyor John Thorpe in 1590 and c. 1604, give us an idea of the layout and scale of the palace, which at its peak of development was comparable in size to Hampton Court and Windsor Castle. It comprised of an outer court, where a number of service buildings were located, including the spicery, pastry and privy bakehouse, and a moated inner or great court, accessed via a stone bridge, constructed in the 1470s.

Around the courtyard stood timber galleries, which gave access to the main residential blocks: the queen's apartments in the west range, and courtiers' lodgings to the east. In the range opposite the inner gatehouse and porter's lodge, stood Edward IV's Great Hall. From the upper end, the monarch could access the main royal apartments – possibly linked to the queen's rooms by a privy gallery – with the lower end leading to the kitchens and a series of smaller service courtyards. Projecting into the main courtyard was Henry VIII's magnificent chapel, running virtually parallel to the Great Hall.

To the south and beyond the moat were the privy gardens, which could be accessed directly from the royal apartments via a small bridge. Three hunting parks, a permanent tiltyard, archery butts and a bowling alley ensured the court was entertained during their stays.

The Philosopher and the Prince

Over its long history, Eltham has welcomed many famous visitors, including the poet Geoffrey Chaucer in 1390, the Byzantine emperor, Manuel Palaeologus, in 1400, the Holy Roman emperor, Sigismund, in 1416, and in 1499, the Dutch philosopher Desiderius Erasmus.

In the autumn of 1499, Erasmus was on his first visit to England and staying at the country house of William Blount, Lord Mountjoy, near Greenwich. On one particular day, Thomas More came to see him and suggested they go for a walk to the next village, where the king's children, with the exception of Prince Arthur, were 'being educated'. Erasmus was presented to the royal children in Edward IV's Great Hall. He later recalled the meeting:

> When we came into the hall, the attendants not only of the palace but also of Mountjoy's household were all assembled. In the midst stood Prince Henry, now nine years old [*sic*], and having already something of royalty in his demeanour, in which there was a certain dignity combined with singular courtesy. On his right was Margaret about eleven years of age, afterwards married to James, King of Scots; and on his left Mary, a child of four. Edmund was an infant in arms. More, with his companion Arnold, after paying his respects to the boy Henry, the same that now is King of England, presented him with some writing. For my part, not having expected anything of the sort, I had nothing to offer, but promised that on another occasion I would in some way declare my duty towards him. Meantime I was angry with More for not having warned me, especially as the boy sent me a little note, while we were at dinner, to challenge something from my pen. I went home, and in the Muses' spite from whom I had been so long divorced, finished the poem within three days.

At such a young age, Henry was already displaying a penchant for theatrical performance. The historian David Starkey summed it up perfectly in his biography of Henry's early years, *Henry: Virtuous Prince*:

> He turned the dais of his grandfather, Edward IV's hall (on which he was surely standing) into a stage, the throng of

attendants into the extras and his sisters and younger brother into the supporting cast.

The Palace's Decline

By the end of the Tudor reign, Eltham Palace was falling into ruin. Elizabeth I's successor, James I, visited the palace in May 1603 and found it 'farre in decay'. He concluded that it was not fit for royalty and embarked on a program of restoration. In spite of the injection of cash, the king visited only infrequently, and its decline continued to accelerate. By 1649, the parliamentary survey declared Eltham to be 'much out of repaire, and soe not tenantable'.

In 1651, it was sold to the Parliamentarian Colonel Nathaniel Rich, who did nothing to alleviate the house's dilapidated state, and instead demolished many of the ancient buildings. John Evelyn toured the former royal residence in 1656, and recorded in his diary, 'Went to see his Majesty's house at Eltham; both the palace and chapel in miserable ruins, the noble wood and park destroyed by Rich the rebel'.

In 1660, Eltham reverted to the Crown. By this time, many of the palace buildings had collapsed or been destroyed, with the exception of the Great Hall and chapel, which survived, albeit in a ruinous state.

For the next 200 years, the once palatial buildings, where kings and queens once dined and royal children played, was tenanted out and used as a farm. In the nineteenth and early twentieth centuries, some repairs were made to the Great Hall, the most significant of these between 1911 and 1914, when the roof of the Great Hall was dismantled and reassembled, with new steel braces supporting the timbers. However, it wasn't until the 1930s, when Stephen and Virginia Courtauld leased the property from the Crown and built a modern mansion on the site, incorporating the medieval Great Hall, that its future was secured.

Visitor Information

Today, Eltham Palace is managed by English Heritage, and open to the public. While there is a car park on site, it is easily accessible from London by train, Mottingham Station being just a 10-minute walk away. Once you arrive at the station, turn left and make your way to the main road, Court Road. Make another left and follow the road until you come across the sign for Eltham Palace on your left. The long driveway leads to the visitor centre, where you'll find a gift shop and café.

Once you have your tickets, exit the visitor centre and follow the path, past the children's play area and rose garden, towards the medieval stone bridge, built by Edward IV in the 1470s. This is the very bridge that visitors to the palace in the sixteenth century would have crossed, and is a lovely place to stop and absorb the history of the site. The area behind you as you face the bridge, was once the site of Eltham's outer court, where various service buildings stood, and beyond the bridge, beneath the modern day turning circle created by the Courtaulds, lies the remains of the medieval inner court.

The highlight of any Tudor enthusiast's visit to Eltham, of course, is the magnificent Great Hall, and while it's tempting to rush through the art deco mansion just to get there, I recommend taking some time to explore the house, with one of the free multimedia guides on offer.

Once you've finished inside, and no doubt spent a significant amount of time marvelling at the beauty of the Great Hall, and picturing a precocious 8-year-old Prince Henry holding court, head back outside to the turning circle.

If you were standing here, facing the hall, in Tudor times, to your left, roughly where the mansion stands today, would have stood the east range of the palace, which contained courtiers' lodgings. Behind you would have risen Henry VIII's chapel, and to your right, the queen's apartments. While there is nothing left to see, above ground, of the chapel – its remains are buried beneath the lawn – it is possible to see remnants of the west range of the royal apartments, which contained the queen's rooms to the north and the king's to the south.

Finally, wander through the many acres of enchanting gardens, where Eltham's medieval past comes charging. Listen carefully and you may just hear the sounds of pounding hooves and splintering lances that once echoed here.

For prices and opening times, visit: www.english-heritage.org.uk/visit/places/eltham-palace-and-gardens

Postcode: SE9 5NP

> Westwards of the Town, the Bishop of London hath his Palace [Fulham], which is an old but good building, with fine gardens.
>
> J. Strype, *A Survey of the Cities of London and Westminster*, 1720

The manor house of Fulham – or, as it's been known since the 1700s, Fulham Palace – has been home to the bishops of London for over 1,000 years. At the beginning of the sixteenth century, it was one of more than twenty manors in Middlesex and the surrounding counties owned by the very wealthy bishops of London and used as a country retreat, to where the bishop and his household would retire over the summer months. Standing in spacious, verdant grounds on the north bank of the River Thames and surrounded by a moat, it was an attractive and much healthier alternative to the crowded and unsanitary streets of London, while still being conveniently close to the City and centre of royal power.

While a bishop's residence is known to have existed on the site since as early as 1141, it was rebuilt in its current location in the thirteenth century, but partially demolished and heavily altered in the 1700s, after Bishop Robinson petitioned the Archbishop of Canterbury to request permission to demolish a number of the buildings that had fallen into disrepair. In his letter he stated that:

> ... the manor-house, or palace, of Fulham was grown very old and ruinous, that it was much too large for the revenues of the bishopric, and that a great part of the building was become useless.

As a result, the palace complex was significantly reduced and altered, and sadly, little is known of the appearance and layout of the original medieval palace.

Touring Fulham Palace Today

The present building has been described as a 'Hampton Court in miniature' because it is partly Tudor and partly Georgian, with a Victorian chapel. If arriving via the main entrance on Bishop's Avenue, look down from the bridge to see part of the moat (filled in from 1921 to 1924) which surrounds the palace grounds. At around 1 mile in length, it is the longest domestic moat in England and forms the boundary of the original palace complex, enclosing an area of approximately 36 acres, 13 of which remain as part of the estate today.

Once across the bridge, note the two nineteenth-century lodges that greet you: the one on your left, as you enter, was built in *c*. 1815, in Gothic style, and the red-brick building opposite in 1893.

Continuing along the main path, the lawn on your right is known as the Paddock, and is believed to be the site of the original twelfth-century residence, rebuilt in its current position in the thirteenth century. A pair of oak gates that date from 1495 give access to the west courtyard, the oldest surviving part of the palace, where the red-brick walls with diamond patterns give away the building's Tudor origin.

It's believed that Richard Fitzjames, Bishop of London from 1506 to 1522, had the four ranges surrounding the quadrangle built on the site of earlier buildings. The range on the east of the courtyard, opposite the main gateway, contains a tower, which somewhat resembles that of the Old Palace, Hatfield. While most of the windows date from the seventeenth century, the glass is largely modern thanks to the bombs that fell nearby the palace during the Second World War. In around 1814, the porch was altered by Bishop Howley and in 1853, the south wall was rebuilt by Bishop Bloomfield, whose coat of arms can be seen over the central doorway. The fountain that stands at the centre of the courtyard is the work of Bishop Butterfield and dates to *c*. 1885. Unfortunately, there is no access to the rooms in the north, west and south ranges of the Tudor quadrangle. However, it is possible to access the oldest room in the palace, built in around 1495, the Great Hall.

The Great Hall

Like much of Fulham Palace, the Great Hall has been altered several times over the centuries. At first glance, there is nothing 'medieval' about the hall, however, above the present ceiling the original timber roof of 1495 survives. We know from the 1647 parliamentary survey of the house that the hall was originally double-storey, and contained two large rooms above the hall with a smaller room on each side. In the mid-eighteenth century, when the present ceiling was inserted to modernise the space, these rooms were removed but the division between the chambers can still be seen in the oak roof.

The Tudor Courtyard, Fulham Palace, 2016. This courtyard is the oldest surviving part of Fulham Palace. It was constructed in the early sixteenth century by Richard Fitzjames, Bishop of London. (Author's collection, by permission of Fulham Palace)

It's in this hall that Bishop Bonner supposedly tortured Protestant prisoners in 1558. In Foxe's *Book of Martyrs* (1563) is a picture which is said to depict Bishop Bonner burning the hand of Thomas Tomkins 'in the hall of that tyrant's house, at Fulham in Middlesex ...'. The hall is also where Queen Elizabeth I may have dined when she visited Bishop Bancroft in 1600 and 1602. According to Strype, referring to an earlier visit made by the queen, she 'misliked nothing [about Fulham palace], but that her lodgings were kept from all good prospect by the thickness of the trees'.

An entry in the Middlesex County Records, dated 9 August 1600, gives details of a robbery that occurred at Fulham Palace during the queen's visit. It's stated that:

> ... on the said day, Arthur Sotherton and Griffin Thomas, both late of London yomen broke into the dwelling-house of Richard the Bishop of London, and there stole a silver salte worth four pounds, of the goods and chattels of the Lady the Queen Elizabeth, the said Queen in her Royal Majesty being then and there at Fullham and in the said house ...

In 1814, the hall was converted into an unconsecrated chapel but later restored to its original use when Bishop Tait built the present chapel in 1866. The Tait Chapel can be accessed via the corridor opposite to the Great Hall.

Historic Rooms & Museum

The rooms today situated around the East Courtyard, including Bishop Sherlock's Room, the Porteus Library, the museum and Bishop Terrick's Rooms, were rebuilt in the eighteenth and nineteenth centuries, on the site of the medieval palace. According to Nikolaus Pevsner, the bishop's lodgings would have originally stood on the north side and the medieval chapel on the east. Sadly, very little else is known about the episcopal palace's original appearance.

While exploring the aforementioned rooms, keep an eye out for the coat of arms of King Henry VIII and Catherine Howard in the Porteus Library, which stands on the site of an eighteenth-century chapel, and the cabinet of medieval and Tudor artefacts in the museum, where undoubtedly the mummified rat will catch your attention!

The Gardens

Take your time exploring the expansive gardens of Fulham Palace, which boast many rare trees. I suggest beginning your tour outside the café and working your way around the palace buildings and gardens, in a clockwise direction. For those of you interested in identifying a particular tree species, I recommend buying the palace's guidebook, where you'll find a map and a list of fifty-nine noteworthy trees to look out for.

While the present landscaping and layout date from the eighteenth and nineteenth centuries, there are some interesting features that will be of particular interest to the Tudor time traveller, including the Holm oak tree that is believed to be over 500 years old! The red-brick wall nearby, and gateway leading into the walled garden, are also Tudor, as are the three bee boles that can be seen in this section of the wall. The weathered coat of arms of Bishop Fitzjames, largely responsible for building the Tudor Courtyard, can be seen above the gateway.

The gardens of Fulham Palace rose to prominence in the late seventeenth and early eighteenth centuries, while in the care of Bishop Compton, a keen student of botany and collector of rare plants. The diarist John Evelyn visited the bishop at Fulham in October 1681, recording in his *Diary* that it was the first time he'd seen a *Sedum arborescens* in flower, which he noted was 'exceedingly beautiful'.

Compton was not, though, the only Bishop of London to take an interest in horticulture. Each year, Bishop Edmund Grindal (1559–70), who established an important botanic garden at Fulham, sent grapes to Queen Elizabeth I. John Strype recorded in the *Life and Acts of Edmund Grindal* that 'the vines at Fulham were of that goodness and perfection beyond others, that the grapes were very acceptable to the Queen'.

Despite being only 6km south-west of central London, the palace grounds are imbued with a sense of peace and tranquility, and continue to offer locals and visitors alike a sanctuary from fast-paced city life. While there is not much of the medieval/Tudor palace left to see, its long and intriguing history, fascinating mixture of architecture and idyllic setting make this a site well worth visiting.

Visitor Information

I visited Fulham Palace on a sunny spring day in April. While the temperatures were still crisp for that time of year, Londoners were out in force, picnicking in the extensive palace grounds, and making the most of the blue skies.

If you are travelling to Fulham Palace on public transport, as I did, the closest underground station is Putney Bridge. It's a short 10-minute walk from the palace. Once you exit the station, turn left and then make a right turn onto Ranelagh Gardens and follow the signs for the 'Thames Walk' towards Bishop's Park.

You'll come to an underground tunnel, which leads into the aforementioned park. The church you see on your right is All Saint's Church, Fulham, where Sir William Butts, Henry VIII's physician, is buried. While his original tomb does not survive, his memorial, a small stone tablet surmounted by a skull, can be found in the south aisle.

Continue walking along and you will come across a gated entry on your right that leads into the palace grounds, it's well sign-posted so you should have no trouble finding it. This entry leads you to the back of the house, through the walled garden and across a large expanse of lawn that in the nineteenth century played host to lavish garden parties of up to 4,000 guests! While this part of the building is obviously Georgian, follow the signs to the main entrance of the house and you will come upon the west or Tudor Courtyard, with its fifteenth-century wooden gates and unmistakable diaper-patterned brickwork, characteristic of the Tudor period. From here you can access the Great Hall, the Georgian rooms and the Victorian chapel, along with the gift shop, museum and café, which offers a wide variety of food and drinks.

If you have time, why not cross to the south side of Putney Bridge and take a walk down Brewhouse Lane, where a blue plaque reminds us that Thomas Cromwell, a prominent figure at the court of Henry VIII, was born nearby.

For opening times and other visitor information, visit Fulham Palace's website at: www.fulhampalace.org

Postcode: SW6 6EA

All Saint's Church, Fulham, 2016. The church's tower was built in the middle of the fifteenth century and is all that remains of the medieval building. (Author's collection)

This yeare, the fyrst daye of December, was arrigned at the Guyld Hall in London Thomas Culpepper, one of the Gentlemen of the Kinges Pryvie Chamber, and Frauncis Dorand [Francis Dereham], gentleman, for high treason against the Kinges Majestie in mysdemeanor with the Quene ...

Charles Wriothesley, Tudor chronicler

Situated in the heart of London's Square Mile, the Guildhall has been the ceremonial and administrative centre of the City of London's local government since around the twelfth century.

The present-day Great Hall was built under the direction of the master mason John Croxtone, on the site of an earlier building, between 1411 and 1440 – its magnificence a testament to the great wealth and power of the Lord Mayor of London during this era. It is the only secular building in the City to have survived both the Great Fire of 1666 and the Blitz, although in both instances it sustained considerable damage.

Like Westminster Hall, the Guildhall was the setting for a number of important state trials in the sixteenth century, including those of Francis Dereham and Thomas Culpeper, both charged with high treason for their alleged affairs with Queen Catherine Howard; Anne Askew, the Protestant martyr; Henry Howard, Earl of Surrey, a first cousin of both Anne Boleyn and Catherine Howard; Lady Jane Grey and her husband, Lord Guildford Dudley, and Thomas Cranmer, Archbishop of Canterbury.

The Trial of Francis Dereham and Thomas Culpeper

In late October 1541, after having just returned home from a long progress to the north of England, an ailing 50-year-old King Henry VIII learnt of his young wife's premarital sexual liaisons with Henry Manox and Francis Dereham, and of her alleged affair with Thomas Culpeper, a gentleman of the king's privy chamber. While at first the king remained sceptical of the

Guildhall, 2016. This was the setting for a number of important state trials in the sixteenth century, including those of Francis Dereham and Thomas Culpeper, both charged with high treason for their alleged affairs with Queen Catherine Howard. (Author's collection)

rumours and ordered an enquiry primarily to protect Catherine Howard's reputation, it soon became clear that the evidence against his 'rose without a thorn' was too damning to ignore.

By the middle of November 1541, Catherine's household had been dismissed and the queen removed from the palace to house arrest at Syon House. Just a fortnight later, on 1 December, Dereham and Culpeper were tried for high treason at the Guildhall. The Tudor chronicler Charles Wriothesley recorded that the Lord Mayor presided over the trial, with the support of the following people:

> ... the Lord Chancellor on his right hand, and the Duke of Norfolk [Catherine's uncle] on his left hand, the Duke of Suffolk, the Lord Privy Seal, the Earls of Sussex, of Hertford, and divers other of the King's Council, with all the judges, sitting there also in commission the same day. [Spelling modernised.]

Both men were found guilty and condemned to be hung, drawn and quartered. The imperial ambassador, Eustace Chapuys, furnishes us with further details of the proceedings, in a letter to the Emperor Charles V:

> All the privy councillors witnessed the trial, which, after a long discussion lasting six hours, ended in the condemnation of the two abovementioned gentlemen [Dereham and Culpepper], who were sentenced to be hung and quartered as traitors. Durem did confess having known the Queen familiarly before she was either betrothed or promised to the King; but said he did not know that there was any wrong in that, inasmuch as they were then engaged to each other. Colpeper persisted in denying the guilt of which he was accused, maintaining that he never solicited or had anything to do with her; on the contrary, it was she who had importuned him through Mme. de Rochefort [Jane Boleyn], requesting him (Colpeper) to go and meet her in a retired place in Lincolnshire, to which she appointed him, and that on that

occasion he (Colpeper) having kept the appointment, she herself told him, as she had on the first instance sent him word through Mme. Rochefort, that she pined for him, and was actually dying of love for his person. It is thought that both will be beheaded to-day. Dame de Rochefort would have been sentenced at the same time had she not, on the third day after her imprisonment, been seized with a fit of madness (frenesi) by which her brain is affected.

On 10 December, both Dereham and Culpeper were executed at Tyburn. The king commuted Culpeper's sentence to beheading, however, Dereham suffered the full traitor's death. Catherine and Lady Rochford met their ends at the Tower of London on 13 February 1542. Only Henry Manox survived the king's wrath, he was questioned, but no further action was taken against him.

Visitor Information

At 152ft long, 50ft wide and 89ft high, the medieval Great Hall is sure to impress. The present roof was designed by Sir Giles Gilbert Scott in 1953, and is the fifth roof to have enclosed this historic building. Around the hall are statues of figures from British history, including Admiral Lord Nelson, the Duke of Wellington and Sir Winston Churchill. Keep an eye out for the statues of Gog and Magog, legendary giants who are said to have founded London. The original Elizabethan statues were destroyed in a fire, and the present-day figures made by David Evans in 1953.

Beneath the Great Hall lies a hidden treasure, the largest medieval crypt in London. The eastern half of the crypt is the oldest part of the Guildhall and believed to date back to the eleventh century,

with the western half dating to the twelfth century. Unfortunately, it is not always open to the public. As the Great Hall is still used for civic or state functions, it too occasionally closes on very short notice, so I recommend phoning ahead of your visit to avoid disappointment.

The Great Hall, the crypt and the other modern rooms which make up the Guildhall complex can all be explored from the comfort of your home by taking the interactive virtual tour on the Guildhall's website.

Finally, in the courtyard in front of the hall is a black circle that marks the outline of the Roman amphitheatre which once stood on the site, remains of which can be seen in the basement of the Guildhall Art Gallery.

The Guildhall is just a short walk from Bank or St Paul's underground stations.

For opening times and other visitor information, please visit: www.cityoflondon.gov.uk/things-to-do/visit-the-city/attractions/guildhall-galleries/Pages/guildhall.aspx

Postcode: EC2V 7HH

Interior of the Great Hall, Guildhall, 2016. (Author's collection, by kind permission of the City of London Corporation)

This palace is situated by the Thames on a very long and wide alluvial plain: it is larger than any other in England so it is commonly – and deservedly – known as 'England's Wateringplace'. This is considered to be the most splendid of the palaces and to be the best for its collection of tapestries.

Excerpt from the diary of Baron Waldstein, who visited England in the summer of 1600

Within the russet-coloured walls of Hampton Court Palace, the past emerges from behind a veil of time – the sights, sounds

and smells evoking memories of an era when this building thrummed with intrigue and power, as the epicentre of politics and the royal Tudor court. For the Tudor time traveller, this is the holy grail of locations; for all the Tudor kings and queens, and prominent personalities of the day have crossed the threshold of Hampton Court Palace, where perhaps their footsteps echo yet ...

The palace we see today is sprawling and magnificent, but it is not all Tudor. At the end of the seventeenth century, William III and Mary II commissioned Sir Christopher Wren to rebuild Hampton Court. The intention was to demolish all the buildings, with the exception of the Great Hall, however, thankfully, both money and time proved scarce, and only part of their ambitious plan was realised.

Wren replaced the Tudor royal apartments with a new baroque palace, completely transforming the south and east façades of Hampton Court, and also re-landscaped the formal gardens. In an ironic twist of fate, neither William nor Mary lived to enjoy their elegant new lodgings: Mary died in 1694, after contracting hemorrhagic smallpox, and in March 1702, William died at Kensington Palace. Although he sustained injuries, including a broken collarbone, in a riding accident at Hampton Court Park (also known as Home Park) just two weeks before his death, it's generally agreed among historians that he died from pneumonia.

The eighteenth century saw the completion of the queen's apartments, begun by Wren, and the addition of the queen's staircase by William Kent. Not long after, in 1737, the royal family – George II and Queen Caroline – accompanied by the court, stayed at the palace for the final time. From 1760 onwards, Hampton Court Palace was divided into grace

Early twentieth-century painting of
Hampton Court Palace by A.R. Quinton.
(Author's collection)

and favour apartments, and opened to the public under Queen Victoria.

Despite the changes made over the years to the original fabric of the buildings, more survives of Hampton Court than of any other Tudor palace, making it a must-see destination for those on the trail of the Tudors.

Thomas Wolsey and Hampton Court Palace

In January 1515, Thomas Wolsey, the newly appointed Archbishop of York and soon to be Lord Chancellor, took a 99-year lease on Hampton Court from the Knights Hospitallers of St John of Jerusalem, who'd first acquired the manor in 1236. Wolsey's new house, which had previously been in the hands

Hampton Court Palace, 2016. Despite the changes made over the years to the original fabric of the buildings, more survives of Hampton Court than of any other Tudor palace. (Author's collection)

of Henry VII's Lord Chamberlain, Sir Giles Daubeney, had been extensively rebuilt in the late fifteenth century and was of a typical late-medieval plan, with the majority of buildings, including a great hall, arranged around a courtyard. Henry VII and Elizabeth of York visited the house not long before the queen's death in 1503, and so it was evidently spacious and luxurious enough to cater for royalty.

It was, however, not grand enough for Cardinal Wolsey, who embarked on a building campaign which would transform Hampton Court into a magnificent, double-courtyard mansion. He built himself sumptuous new lodgings, as well as luxurious new apartments for Henry VIII, Katherine of Aragon and Princess Mary on the site of the present-day east range of Clock Court. Wolsey extended Daubeney's kitchens and created new courtyards, residential apartments, galleries and splendid gardens – an ostentatious display of his wealth and power.

In 1529, Henry VIII took possession of Hampton Court, and continued the work started by the now disgraced cardinal, making extensive alterations and embellishments to the palace complex, as attested to by the 6,500 pages of work accounts that survive in the Public Record Office. By the time of Henry VIII's death in 1547, Hampton Court Palace was the ultimate royal pleasure palace, boasting magical gardens, a vast hunting park of around 1,100 acres, tennis courts, bowling alleys and a permanent tiltyard. It was a palace built to impress and dazzle his subjects and visitors, a spectacular manifestation of Tudor royal power and magnificence.

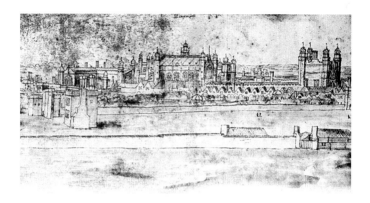

View of the north of Hampton Court Palace made by Anton van den Wyngaerde in 1558. In the foreground on the left, are the banqueting houses, behind which is the Tudor tennis court, the Great Hall in the centre and the outer gatehouse on the right. (By the kind permission of the Stationery Office)

A Walk Back in Time

The main entrance to the palace today is via the west front, through Wolsey's great gatehouse, reduced in height in the eighteenth century from five to three storeys. Pause for a moment on the moat bridge while facing the central gateway surmounted with the arms of Henry VIII, the turrets you see were originally crowned with lead onion domes, as seen in Anthonis van den Wyngaerde's view of the palace from the north, made in around 1558. The two terracotta roundels of the heads of the Roman emperors Tiberius and Nero are Victorian additions, but were probably originally from the Holbein Gate at Whitehall.

The ten heraldic beasts, which line the bridge leading to the central gateway were installed in 1911, to replace the original Tudor beasts destroyed in the reign of King William III. Unlike their Tudor predecessors, the beasts we see today are unpainted. Among them: the crowned lion of England, supporting a shield bearing the impaled arms of Henry VIII and

Jane Seymour; the greyhound, a favoured Tudor beast and a symbol of loyalty and celerity; and the mighty Tudor dragon.

When standing facing Wolsey's gatehouse, the range you see projecting out to your right once contained the 'common jakes', later known as 'The Great House of Easement', a multiple garderobe, which originally emptied into the moat. The range to your left was the 'Back Gate', which allowed access to the main kitchen buildings and contained, among other offices and lodgings, the Counting House, the administrative hub of the royal household.

Make your way into Base Court and prepare to be propelled back into the sixteenth century. This area of the palace remains much as it was when Wolsey built it to provide luxury accommodation for a large number of guests. The north and south ranges contained in total thirty, two-room suites and three single lodgings all accessed via an internal gallery that wrapped around three sides of the courtyard. This revolutionary design allowed guests to move between rooms without being impacted by the weather. A large three-room suite was located over the gatehouse.

Each of the guest rooms contained a garderobe and fireplace, and those in the north and south ranges contained ample windows that overlooked the gardens. Apart from being spacious and well lit, they were also very richly furnished and well stocked, as seen in George Cavendish's very detailed description of the arrival of a French embassy to Hampton Court in 1527, recorded in his biography of Cardinal Wolsey:

> ... they returned again to Hampton Court, and every of them conveyed to his chamber severally having in them great fires and wine ready to refresh them, remaining there until their supper was ready, and the chambers where they should sup were ordered in due form ... and whilst they were in conversation and other pastimes, all their liveries were served to their chambers. Every chamber had a basin and a ewer of silver and some clean gilt and some parcel gilt, and some two great pots of silver in like manner, and one pot at the least with wine

and beer, a bowl or goblet, and a silver pot to drink beer, a silver candlestick or two, both with white lights and yellow lights of three sizes of wax, and a staff torch, a fine manchet, and a cheat loaf of bread. Thus was every chamber furnished throughout the house ...

The centrepiece of the courtyard today is the 4m-high recreated Tudor wine fountain that was unveiled in April 2010 and inspired by a number of historic sources, including the *Field of the Cloth of Gold* painting created in the 1540s and displayed in the 'Young Henry VIII' exhibition at the palace.

In its heyday, Hampton Court was home to a number of fountains, also known as conduits, including one that stood in Base Court and a larger and more elaborate one in Clock Court. Baron Waldstein described the latter in his diary after a visit to Hampton Court in the summer of 1600:

This quadrangle [Clock Court] is paved with squared stone and in the centre there is a fountain with a golden crown around the top of it: above this stands a gilt figure of Justice. The fountain spurts its water out of marble columns.

Apart from water, on special occasions, such as the coronation of a new monarch, the conduits also ran with wine, something the present fountain is also engineered to do.

The Great Hall

As you make your way towards the Great Hall, take note of the fan vault beneath the Middle Gate, today known as Anne Boleyn's Gateway. It's decorated with the entwined initials of Henry VIII and Anne Boleyn. The gatehouse was heavily restored in the late nineteenth century, and while the ceiling dates to this period, it's a close copy of the original Tudor vaulting.

Pause for a moment at the top of the staircase, the site of the processional stair in Tudor times, and take note of Katherine of Aragon's personal badge, the pomegranates, which decorate the doorway leading into the buttery. Make your way into the grand and beautiful Great Hall, begun by Henry VIII in 1532. It's the largest room in the palace, measuring around 32m long, 12m wide and over 18m high. As the entrance to Henry's state apartments, it needed to be suitably impressive and magnificent, hence the splendid and richly decorated hammerbeam roof, which in Tudor times would have been brightly painted.

At the lower end of the hall, the Tudor oak screen carved with the entwined initials of Henry and Anne Boleyn, which can also be seen on the ceiling, separates the hall from the buttery, and would have originally supported a minstrel's gallery. Rather than the timber floor we see today, the hall was originally paved with tiles, and a stone hearth stood in the centre of the room, the smoke escaping through a lavishly decorated louvre above.

The beautiful Flemish tapestries of the *Story of Abraham* that today line the walls were commissioned by Henry VIII and woven by Willem Kempaneer in the 1540s with silver and gold thread. Time has dulled the tapestries but it's still possible to get a sense of how striking they would have been when first produced.

The Great Watching Chamber and Horn Room

The Great Chamber, remodelled by Henry VIII in the mid-1530s, was the outermost chamber of Henry's state apartments (a function occasionally served by the Great Hall), and as such was a room in which courtiers could gather with relative freedom. It came under the control of the Lord Chamberlain, whose department was also responsible for supervising the Great Hall and Presence Chamber.

During Henry's reign, the Great Chamber also served as a dining room for courtiers 'above the rank of a baron', and, according to Simon Thurley, was where 'almost all the normal intercourse of the court took place'. It's likely that it was to this room that Sir Thomas Wriothesley summonsed Catherine Howard's household on 13 November 1541, before dismissing them and ordering the young queen's removal from Hampton Court, to house arrest at Syon House.

The door directly to your right as you enter the room from the hall roughly marks the site of the entryway to Henry's presence chamber and state apartments, which no longer exist. The king's Yeomen of the Guard, dressed in red uniforms and armed with long pikes, would have guarded the door around the clock, and only permitted entry to those with the proper authority. Beyond the Presence Chamber stood a succession of private rooms, including the privy and withdrawing chambers, which came under the control of the Groom of the Stool. The garderobe created for the king's yeomen, who slept in the Great Chamber at night, still survives.

While the room today owes much of its appearance to later restorations, the beautiful ceiling decorated with the arms of Henry VIII and Jane Seymour, and the tapestries, date to the sixteenth century.

The Horn Room was originally where servants waited before taking food into the Great Hall and Great Watching Chamber. The staircase leads up from the kitchens, and while the balustrade is Victorian, the original and well-worn Tudor oak steps survive.

The room acquired its name when the palace was partially rebuilt during the reign of William III, at which time the antlers and horns that had previously decorated the Tudor galleries were taken down and stored here.

No doubt you will already have noticed the life-size portrait of a porter who served Elizabeth I, which hangs on the wall. I'm sure you'll be just as amazed as the author was by his enormous stature!

The Council Chamber, Haunted Gallery and Chapel Royal

As you leave the Great Watching Chamber, and follow the great processional route that led from the king's state apartments to the magnificent double-storey chapel, note the pages' chamber on your right, furnished as it may have appeared in the 1540s. Take your time admiring the many Tudor portraits which decorate the gallery, including a wonderful portrait by an unknown artist of a young boy looking out from behind a window, painted between 1550 and 1560.

Dressed in plain dark clothes, a velvet cap and ruff, the boy stares cheekily out at you from behind a casement, his right finger tapping on the glass, enticing you to engage with him. His left hand is poised on the window's ledge, and appears ready to throw the window open. As you look at him and try to imagine what those mischievous eyes saw, it dawns on you that you've become the subject of observation, rather than the observer.

Continue along the gallery towards the Council Chamber, built by Henry VIII in *c.* 1529 and opened to the public for the first time in 2009. Between 1540 and 1547, there were around nineteen privy councillors (rising to around fifty under Mary I), who met virtually every day to advise the king on anything from foreign policy to the day-to-day running of the court, and would have done so in this very room when in residence at Hampton Court. Just think of the heated debates that would have taken place here, and of all the historic decisions made within these walls.

The second half of the gallery is known traditionally as the Haunted Gallery, as it's said to be home to Catherine Howard's screaming spectre. Legend has it that after Henry learned of his young wife's pre-marital sexual liaisons and had her confined to her apartments, she broke free from her captors, and, knowing that the king was at prayer in the chapel, ran down the corridor in a final desperate attempt to reach her husband

and plead for mercy. She was, however, quickly restrained and dragged back to her apartments in a frenzy of terror, and was executed at the Tower of London on 13 February 1542.

Her ghost is said to replay this final frantic dash, with many guests and staff alike reporting strange goings-on in this area of the palace. Over the years, people have reported a sense of uneasiness and dread in the gallery, others have heard eerie screams, and some visitors have become dizzy, disoriented and, on occasions, even fainted. One man contacted me personally to share his story of being grabbed around the neck by spectral hands!

As much as I love a good ghost story, there is no documentary evidence to confirm that the event ever took place. In fact, it seems likely that Catherine knew nothing of the predicament she was in until the king had departed Hampton Court, only then ordering her confinement. Even so, there is an undeniable atmosphere of mystery in this gallery.

Spooky stories aside, the Haunted Gallery is also home to paintings from the Royal Collection, including portraits of Henry VII and Elizabeth of York and *The Family of Henry VIII*, made in *c*. 1545 by an unknown artist. The painting is set in Whitehall Palace, and shows Henry with his third wife, Jane Seymour, who died at Hampton Court in 1537, and his children, Mary, Elizabeth and Edward. Adorning the neck of the young Elizabeth is an 'A' necklace, which may have belonged to her mother, Anne Boleyn.

From the Haunted Gallery, visitors can access the royal pew, the upper storey of the exquisite Chapel Royal built by Cardinal Wolsey and modernised by Henry VIII, which overlooks the main body of the chapel. From 1535 onwards, the pew was divided into two large rooms, known as the 'Queen's Holyday Closet' and the 'King's Holyday Closet', where the king and queen worshipped separately on Sundays and feast days, hence the name 'holyday'. On the feast of Epiphany on 6 January, the king would wear his crown and robes and process to the chapel to hear Mass. The original crown does not survive, however a replica is currently on display in the royal pew. At all other times, the king worshipped privately in his privy closet, located between his presence and privy chambers.

On 15 October 1537, Henry and Jane Seymour's son, Prince Edward, was baptised in the chapel. Tragically, less than two weeks later, his mother died following post-natal complications and celebrations quickly turned to mourning. Henry ordered that Jane's heart and entrails be buried in the chapel, where her body lay in state before being moved to St George's Chapel, Windsor, where she was buried on 12 November 1537, just one month after having given birth to Henry's longed-for heir.

In July 1543, Henry married his sixth and final wife, Katherine Parr, in the Queen's Privy Closet at Hampton Court Palace, in the presence of around twenty guests, including his daughters, Mary and Elizabeth. A copy of their wedding certificate is on display in the Holyday Closet.

The Cumberland Art Gallery and Wolsey Closet

The art gallery is housed in the newly restored Cumberland Suite, designed by the eminent English architect William Kent, for George II's son, William Augustus, Duke of Cumberland, and completed by about 1734. On display are some magnificent artworks, principally from the Royal Collection, including masterpieces by Holbein, van Dyck and Rembrandt.

As you admire the work of these renowned artists, keep in mind that the Cumberland Suite was built on the site of the first Tudor state apartments, originally constructed by Cardinal Wolsey to house Princess Mary on the ground floor, Henry on the first floor and Queen Katherine directly above him. Think back to the closed door at the far end of the Great Watching Chamber, this once led into Henry's presence chamber, now greatly altered and inaccessible to the public, and onto the king's most private rooms, including his dining and privy chamber.

Henry later refurbished these lodgings and ordered that lavish new rooms be built for his second wife, Anne Boleyn, overlooking the sweeping parkland to the east, however, these were not completed until early 1536 and so Anne Boleyn would have stayed in the old queen's rooms, designed for her predecessor, while awaiting their completion. She was executed in May 1536, before ever getting the chance to enjoy her new apartments.

The flurry of construction work kept Henry and his new wife, Jane Seymour, away from Hampton Court until May 1537, at which time the bewildered – and no doubt exhausted – craftsmen were ordered by the king to begin work on rebuilding and extending the newly completed queen's apartments. Perhaps Queen Jane did not feel comfortable staying in rooms designed for her former mistress. In any case, Jane too was forced to use the same old lodgings used by Katherine and Anne, and gave birth to Prince Edward in one of the rooms on 12 October 1537. Jane would never fully recover from Edward's birth, dying just twelve days later.

The entrance to the suite of rooms used by Henry's first three queens survives, albeit in a heavily altered state, and is today used as a meeting and training room, and not open to the public. A fireplace decorated with Cardinal Wolsey's badges and mottoes hints at the room's Tudor past.

Before leaving this area of the palace, be sure to visit the Wolsey Closet, just beyond the Cumberland Suite, as it allows us a glimpse into what a Tudor 'closet', or small room, would have looked like. Although it was heavily restored in the nineteenth century, part of the gilded wood and leather mache ceiling, which dates to the late 1530s and is decorated with the Tudor rose and Prince of Wales feathers, has remained *in situ*. The painted panels date from the sixteenth century but are not original to the room.

The Wolsey Rooms & Renaissance Picture Gallery

The Wolsey Rooms formed part of Cardinal Wolsey's private apartments in the 1520s, and were later refurbished for Princess Mary. Like so much of the palace, these rooms were altered and restored in the eighteenth and nineteenth centuries, however, a number of original Tudor features survive, including sixteenth-century linenfold panelling and Tudor fireplaces.

The adjacent Renaissance Picture Gallery and the Wolsey rooms are home to many wonderful sixteenth- and seventeenth-century paintings, including portraits of Anne Boleyn, Henry VIII and Katherine of Aragon.

The Tudor Kitchens

The enormous Tudor kitchens at Hampton Court are a highlight of any visit, and at various times throughout the year are home to live cookery events, where historical chefs bring the 500-year-old kitchens to life by preparing traditional Tudor meals in front of a roaring fire.

Henry VIII extended the kitchens in around 1530 to cater for the 600–800 members of court entitled to eat twice per day in the Great Hall and Great Watching Chamber. In their heyday, they covered around 3,000 square feet and were manned by a staff of 200.

In addition to the main household kitchens, there were also the privy kitchens where the king and queen's own cooks prepared the royal dishes. As a side note, the Privy Kitchen Café is housed in what was once Elizabeth I's privy kitchen.

Today, visitors are free to explore what survives of Henry VIII's great kitchens, including the remains of the Tudor boiling house, the cellars and Fish Court, a narrow courtyard around which once stood a number of different kitchen offices, including the pastry house, flesh larder and fish larder. As you exit the kitchens into Serving Place, be sure not to miss the dressers, where special dishes were garnished before being served to the senior courtiers.

In quiet moments between tourist groups, there is a sense of timelessness in this area of the palace. Particularly in the North Cloister, the passage that leads to the cellars, where it feels possible, or somehow inevitable, that if you remained there long enough you would come face to face with a harried Tudor servant, en route to deliver food to the courtiers dining upstairs.

The Palace Gardens

Hampton Court Palace boasts over 60 acres of formal gardens and more than 650 acres of historic parkland that is home to a large variety of wildlife, including 300 fallow deer, said to be descendants of Henry VIII's original deer herd.

Sir Giles Daubeney enclosed 300 acres of land in what is now Bushy Park, creating Hampton Court's first hunting park. Cardinal Wolsey, never one to be outdone, followed suit by enclosing an even larger area of land to the east of the palace, the present-day Hampton Court Park. He was also the first to build ornamental gardens at the palace, however, it was Henry VIII who, from 1529 onwards, established the gardens that would be greatly lauded and praised. One such admirer was Baron Waldstein who after visiting the palace in the summer of 1600, noted:

> This [the garden] is especially interesting because of its many avenues and also for the large number of growing plants shaped into animals, in fact they even had sirens, centaurs, sphinxes, and other fabulous poetic creatures portrayed here in topiary work.

View of the south of Hampton Court Palace made by Anton van den Wyngaerde in 1558. (By kind permission of the Stationery Office)

The gardens to the south of the palace comprised of the privy garden, designed to be enjoyed from the ground and from the galleries above; the mount garden, which boasted, among other features, a spectacular arbour, and to the west of the privy garden, the pond yard, which contained three ponds that were both ornamental and used for breeding and storing fish.

To the north of the palace stood the privy orchard and a great orchard, separated by the palace moat but linked by a drawbridge. The privy orchard was home to a bowling alley and nearby, on the east front of the palace, stood an indoor tennis court. Henry later completed the entertainment quarter by building a permanent tiltyard on land adjacent to the great orchard.

This layout has over the years been greatly altered to cater for changing tastes in garden design, however, there remain several features of interest to the Tudor time traveller. The sunken pond gardens were the original Tudor ponds, and the Knot Garden and the gardens in Chapel Court were laid out to show the types of gardens Henry may have planted at Hampton Court. If weather permits, spend some time exploring Hampton Court Park, used for hunting and riding in Tudor times. If at the end of the day you're in need of refreshment, head for the Tiltyard Café, built adjacent to the only surviving of Henry's five tiltyard towers, constructed as viewing galleries and banqueting houses.

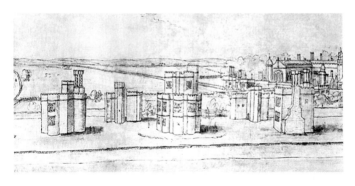

Hampton Court Palace's Tiltyard Towers, used as banqueting houses, from a drawing by Anton van den Wyngaerde made in 1558. (By kind permission of the Stationery Office)

In 1599, the Swiss diarist and physician Thomas Platter extolled, 'Hampton Court is the finest and most magnificent royal edifice to be found in England...', and after more than 400 years, it continues to captivate our hearts and imaginations.

Visitor Information

Hampton Court Palace is easily accessible from London. South West Trains operate regular services from London Waterloo Station. If visiting the palace in the summer, you might like to follow in the footsteps of the Tudor kings and queens and travel to the palace by riverboat. Keep in mind, though, that the journey from Westminster can take up to four hours, depending on the tides, and so will not allow for a full day's visit. For more information, contact Westminster Passenger Services: www.wpsa.co.uk

Hampton Court Palace is managed by the Historic Royal Palaces.

For detailed visitor information, visit their website at www.hrp.org.uk/hampton-court-palace

Postcode: KT8 9AU

A great part of this Palace at Westminster was once againe burnt in the yeare 1512.

John Stow, *Survey of London*, 1598

Standing in the heart of Westminster, the Jewel Tower, known originally as the Jewel House, is one of four remaining sections of the medieval Palace of Westminster to survive the fire of 16 October 1834, which left much of the ancient palace in ruins. While a royal residence is known to have existed in the area since about the first half of the eleventh century, it wasn't until the thirteenth century onwards that the Palace of Westminster became the principal residence of the English monarchy, and home of the law courts and various other government departments.

Building of the Jewel Tower

The Jewel Tower, constructed between 1365 and 1366 during the reign of King Edward III, stood at the south-west corner of the medieval Palace of Westminster, located on the north bank of the River Thames, next to Westminster Abbey. The year-long building project was overseen by Henry Yevele, an experienced builder, who had under his direction a team of masons and other leading craftsmen, including glaziers, plasterers and tilers.

The tower was intended as a repository for the royal household's most valuable and precious possessions, including jewels, plate and textiles. Thus, in order to protect the immeasurable treasures it would house, it was built in a corner of the king's garden, which lay within the privy or private palace, where the royal apartments were located. This was well away from the main entrance gateway in the north, and the more public precinct of the palace, centred in and around the

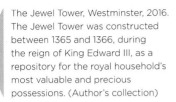

The Jewel Tower, Westminster, 2016. The Jewel Tower was constructed between 1365 and 1366, during the reign of King Edward III, as a repository for the royal household's most valuable and precious possessions. (Author's collection)

enormous Great Hall (today known as Westminster Hall) built by William II between 1097 and 1099, which still stands today, albeit in an altered state.

Its secluded position was not its only protective feature. The entire palace was surrounded by a wall, which formed its boundary, along which were built various gateways and towers, including the aforementioned entrance or great gateway, and the Jewel Tower. The latter projected beyond the precinct walls, an ingenious design that ensured it did not encroach too far upon the king's garden, and as such was protected by a water-filled moat that opened up into the Thames. A nearby gateway led to a landing stage from where items from the Jewel Tower could be loaded onto barges and transported to other royal residences, as required.

Once finished, the tower consisted of three main floors linked by a spiral staircase, each containing a large rectangular room and a smaller adjoining chamber in a turret. The upper two floors were used to store items held by the royal wardrobe, with the more valuable items probably stored on the top floor, in locked wooden chests. On the ground floor, the keeper of the king's jewels would conduct his business and meet with other household officials, with the smaller adjacent chamber serving as his private withdrawing room.

Keeper of the King's Jewels

The person in charge of supervising the contents of the new tower was William Sleaford. He used the title of 'Keeper of the Wardrobe in the Privy Palace of Westminster' or 'Keeper of the jewels and gold and silver vessels', but over time the title for this role varied. It was the keeper's job to ensure that all items housed in the tower were properly recorded. Details including the condition of items – and, importantly, their weight – were noted, as indicators of their value. The keeper was also responsible for lending out items for use at other royal residences or in banquets, and accepting their return, noting any breakages that might need repairing.

From the late fourteenth century onwards, a large variety of items were housed in the tower, many of which were pieces of silver plate, including serving dishes, goblets, saucers, spoons, ewers and plates. They were often elaborately decorated, like

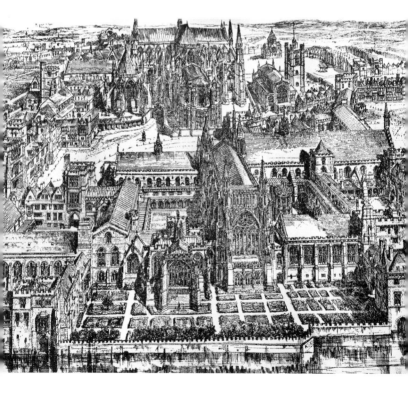

the following item recorded as being a gift from Edward III to his son the Duke of Cambridge:

> A silver spice-plate, gilded all over and enamelled above on the inside with a castle and a damsel chastising a wodewose ...

The fate of the Jewel Tower was inextricably linked to that of the Privy Palace. As long as the royal family remained in residence, its use remained as originally intended. The sixteenth century, however, brought with it changes, and a new function for the old tower.

The Tudor Period

The Elizabethan historian and antiquarian John Stow recorded in his *Survey of London*, published in 1598, that:

> A great part of this Palace at Westminster was once againe burnt in the yeare 1512. the 4. of Henry the eight, since which time, it hath not beene reedified: onely the great Hall, with the offices neare adioyning, are kept in good reparations, and serueth as afore, for feastes at Coronations, Arraignments of great persons charged with treasons, keeping of the Courts of iustice, &c. But the Princes haue beene lodged in other places about the city, as at Baynards Castle, at Bridewell, and White hall, sometime called Yorke place, and sometime at S. Iames.

A reconstruction of Tudor Westminster, viewed from the east, illustrated by H.W. Brewer. Westminster Abbey and St Margaret's Church can be seen in the background. (Author's collection)

According to an earlier entry in the *Survey*, this was not the first time the palace had burnt, and it would not be the last. In 1299, a 'vehement fire' had consumed a number of the buildings, however these were later repaired, and the palace returned to royal favour. It would not enjoy the same good fortune this time around. The Palace of Westminster's time as a principal royal residence had come to an end, and Greenwich Palace became the king's favoured house, until 1529, when Henry acquired York Place, later renamed Whitehall Palace, following Cardinal Wolsey's downfall.

As noted above, after the fire, when 'about the city', the king also lodged at places like Baynard's Castle, Bridewell Palace and sometimes St James' Palace, although in the case of the latter, this would not have been possible until the 1530s, as construction on the Tudor palace, built on the site of a former leper hospital, only began in 1531.

After the court's departure from Westminster, most of the king's jewels and plate were moved elsewhere, and the fourteenth-century tower became a store for unused and unwanted items. By the time of Henry VIII's death in January 1547, it was home to a hodgepodge of royal belongings, including clothes, furniture and bed linen.

By the end of the sixteenth century, the Jewel Tower had become a store for the records of the House of Lords, where they remained until the mid-nineteenth century.

'Stuff in the Old Jewel House at Westminster' in 1547

Six months after the death of King Henry VIII, a formal inventory of his moveable property was drawn up. In this fascinating and hefty document, there appears a list of the 'stuff' being stored in 'tholde Juelhous' at the time. Among the hundreds of items recorded, appear the following:

> Item a greate babye lying in a boxe of wood having a
> gowne of white clothe of siluer and a kirtle of grene

vellat the gowne teyed with smale aglettes of golde and a smale payer of beades of golde and a smale cheyne and a coller aboute the necke of golde.

Item twoo litle babies in a boxe of wood one of theym having a gowne of crymsen satten and thother a gowne of white vellat.

It's possible that these elaborately dressed 'babies' or dolls, had once belonged to a royal child, perhaps Princesses Mary or Elizabeth? A very similar doll appears in a portrait of Lady Arabella Stuart, painted in 1577. Other items of interest include:

Item one lyllye pott wrought with the nedle and a branche of roses white and redd with a white fawcon crowned vppon the topp of the same braunche likewise wrought with the nedle.

Item one payer of Sleves of white satten enbrawdred [embroidered] over with pirled golde acornes and honysocles teyed with tenne payer of aglettes of golde.

The first of these items begs the question, did it once belong to Queen Anne Boleyn, a skilled needlewoman, whose badge was a crowned white falcon alighting on white and red roses? Was it unceremoniously stored and forgotten after her downfall, or hidden away by one of the former queen's loyal supporters, desperate to save some token of their beloved mistress?

The second item, a pair of lady's sleeves, is embroidered with acorns and honeysuckles, a motif adopted by Henry VIII and Anne Boleyn during their relationship, and one that regularly appeared on palace furnishings. This too may have some connection to the fallen queen, although there is no conclusive evidence to prove it.

Other items include: 'a gown of crimson satin with a cape embroidered with gold and furred with black genets', a description that calls to mind Holbein's portrait of Queen

Jane Seymour, who's dressed in a similar gown; 'one walking staff having a cross upon the upper end of black horn ...'; 'ten chamber pots of pewter'; 'one little ship coffer covered with velvet and garnished with copper plate' and 'one great steel looking glass covered with crimson velvet embroidered with damask gold and garnished with small pearls'.

The Fire of 1834

On 16 October 1834, a devastating fire, which started underneath the House of Lords, spread and consumed the Palace of Westminster. Luckily for the Jewel Tower, the prevailing wind was on its side, and blew the flames away from the tower and its neighbour Westminster Abbey.

The Palace of Westminster, more commonly known today as the Houses of Parliament, was eventually rebuilt on the site of its medieval predecessor, incorporating those parts of the palace that had not been completely destroyed, namely Westminster Hall, the Chapel of St Mary Undercroft, and directly above, the Chapel of St Stephen (now St Stephen's Hall) and its cloisters.

Visitor Information

The Jewel Tower is located on Abingdon Street, opposite the southern end of the Houses of Parliament, and is best accessed by public transport, as there is no parking on site. If arriving at Westminster Underground Station (just a short walk away from the Jewel Tower), once you've exited the station – and no doubt joined the other throngs of tourists snapping away at Big Ben – turn right, walking away from the famous London landmark. On your right, you'll pass St Stephen's Tavern, well worth a visit if you have the time. Apart from the attractive

Victorian interiors, they serve a small but reasonably priced menu, for this part of town.

Continue walking along until you reach a set of lights. Turn left and make your way past the Houses of Parliament, towards the Victoria Tower. Directly opposite stands the Jewel Tower, which is now in the care of English Heritage and open to the public. An informative exhibition highlights the tower's

Victoria Tower, Palace of Westminster, 2016, as seen from Victoria Tower Gardens. (Author's collection)

history and changing function over the years. Be sure to explore the area surrounding the tower and try to imagine the king's private garden and sprawling medieval palace spilling out before you.

For prices and opening times, visit: www.english-heritage.org.uk/visit/places/jewel-tower

For more information on St Stephen's Tavern, visit: www.ststephenstavern.co.uk

Postcode: SW1P 3JX

> The seventh day of the aforementioned month of November, the Princess [Katherine of Aragon] on her behalf took her journey to Chertsey and there lodged all night, and from thence towards Lambeth ... where she continued unto such season as her entering into the City of London ...

> From *The Receyt of the Ladie Kateryne*

Situated on the south bank of the River Thames, across from Westminster Palace, Lambeth Palace has been a London residence of the Archbishops of Canterbury since the thirteenth century. Construction commenced on the palace buildings during the tenure of Archbishop Hubert Walter, in the late twelfth century, however, it wasn't until the following century, during the time of Archbishop Stephen Langton – believed to be the first archbishop to live at Lambeth – that the palace's most important rooms were built. These included the archbishop's private apartments, the chapel, Great Chamber and Great Hall. Morton's Tower, the distinctly Tudor, red-brick gatehouse that greets visitors today, was added in the 1490s.

Lambeth Palace Highlights

Over the centuries, the palace buildings have been altered and added to by successive archbishops, to cater for changes in taste and purpose, and also as a result of damage sustained during the English Civil War, at which time the medieval Great Hall was demolished, and more recently, during the Second World War, when the roof of the chapel was destroyed by incendiary bombs. Many of the medieval and Tudor buildings that survived the civil unrest of the seventeenth century were pulled down in the nineteenth century, to make way for a new residential suite for the archbishop and his family. Thankfully,

some of the original buildings survive, albeit in an altered/ restored state. These include the Tudor gatehouse, Chichele's Tower (also known as Lollard's Tower), the Guard Room (former Great Chamber), chapel and crypt.

As Lambeth Palace continues to serve as the London residence of the Archbishop of Canterbury and his family, these rooms, with the exception of Morton's Tower and Chichele's Tower which are not open to the public, can only be visited on a guided tour, or on one of several open days held throughout the year.

The Guard Room

The Guard Room, which is believed to date from the fourteenth century, served as the Great Chamber in Tudor times. This was the principal reception room of a Tudor palace, where the archbishop would have met and entertained important guests, and conducted much of his daily business. Perhaps it was in this very room, that Thomas Cranmer, Archbishop of Canterbury from 1533 to 1555, signed Henry VIII and Katherine Parr's marriage licence, dated 'Lambeth, 10 July 1543'. As the second largest room of the palace, after the Great Hall, the Great Chamber would have been used for a variety of ceremonies, and as a dining room for household officials. At night, it may have also provided accommodation for junior household staff.

Edward Blore, a leading architect employed to design the new residential wing for Archbishop William Howley, restored the room between 1829 and 1830, and so much of what we see today dates from that period, including all of the walls. The magnificent arch-braced roof, though, is an exception. It dates from when the room was first constructed in the fourteenth century.

Morton's Tower, Lambeth Palace, Westminster, 2016. (Author's collection)

While admiring the outstanding medieval craftsmanship, and the many portraits lining the walls, keep in mind that it was probably in this room that, on Monday, 13 April 1534, Sir Thomas More was asked to swear the Oath of Supremacy before the king's commissioners, acknowledging Henry VIII as supreme head of the English Church. More refused, and was eventually sent to the Tower of London, from where he wrote a letter to his eldest daughter, Margaret Roper. What follows is an extract from this letter:

When I was before the Lords at Lambeth, I was the first that was called in, albeit, Master Doctor the Vicar of Croydon was come before me, and divers others. After the cause of my sending for, declared unto me (whereof I somewhat marveled in my mind, considering that they sent for no more temporal men but me), I desired the sight of the oath, which they shewed me under the great Seal. Then desired I the sight of the Act of the Succession, which was delivered me in a printed roll. After which read secretly by myself, and the oath considered with the act, I shewed unto them that my purpose was not to put any fault either in the act or any man that made it, or in the oath or any man that sware it, nor to condemn the conscience of any other man. But as for myself in good faith my conscience so moved me in the matter, that though I would not deny to swear to the succession, yet unto the oath that there was offered me I could not swear without the jeoparding of my soul to perpetual damnation. And that if they doubted whether I did refuse the oath only for the grudge of my conscience, or for any other fantasy, I was ready therein to satisfy them by mine oath. Which if they trusted not, what should they be the better to give me any oath? And if they trusted that I would therein swear true, then trusted I that of their goodness they would not move me to swear the oath that they offered me, perceiving that for to swear it was against my conscience.

More spent fourteen months imprisoned at the Tower of London, before being beheaded on Tower Hill. As you stand in the Guard Room today, it's difficult not to marvel at the fact that once, in this very room, a number of the who's who of Tudor history, including the king's principal secretary, Thomas Cromwell, the Lord Chancellor, Thomas Audley and the Archbishop of Canterbury, Thomas Cranmer, tried to convince Sir Thomas More to set aside his conscience and deny the authority of the pope.

The Crypt and Chapel

Described by the renowned architectural historian, Nikolaus Pevsner, as 'one of the best preserved medieval vaults in London', the crypt is one of the oldest parts of Lambeth Palace, completed in around 1220. Today, it functions as a chapel, although it was probably originally used as a storage room for beer and wine.

Directly above the crypt is the chapel, which also dates to the thirteenth century, however, unlike the crypt, it has been extensively altered over the years. The marble chequered floor and oak screen were installed in the seventeenth century, while the roof and the stained glass date from the twentieth century. In front of the altar, a white tile marks the final resting place of Matthew Parker, who served as a chaplain to Queen Anne Boleyn, and later as Archbishop of Canterbury under Elizabeth I.

The Great Hall and Library

The Great Hall stands on the site of the medieval hall that Cranmer and his contemporaries would have known. Today, it houses much of Lambeth Palace's library, an extensive collection of around 200,000 printed books and more than 4,500 manuscripts, 600 of which are medieval. Among the treasures housed here, are a Gutenberg Bible printed in 1455, a contemporary copy of the warrant for the execution of Mary,

Queen of Scots and two volumes of contemporary papers relating to Henry VIII's divorce proceedings against Katherine of Aragon.

Interestingly, it was at Lambeth Palace that a 15-year-old Katherine stayed for several nights, before making her formal entry into London on 12 November 1501, and where, thirty-two years later, her husband's marriage to Anne Boleyn would be declared valid in 'a certain well-known high gallery in the manor of Lambeth, on Wednesday, 28 May 1533'.

Katherine, though, was not the only member of the Tudor royal family to enjoy the archbishop's hospitality. Between January and March 1514, the court spent more than thirty days at Lambeth Palace. Undoubtedly, the Great Hall served as a backdrop to many lavish banquets and courtly entertainments, including the creation of two dukes and two earls on 2 February. We find recorded in the State Papers that on Candlemas Day, 1514:

> ... the Earl of Surrey, Sir Thomas Howard, senior, Earl Marshal and Treasurer of England, was created Duke of Norfolk; the Viscount Lisle, Sir Charles Brandon, late marshal of the King's army, was created Duke of Suffolk; the Lord Howard, Sir Th. Howard the younger, Admiral of England, was created Earl of Surrey; the Lord Herbert, Sir Charles Somersett, Lord Chamberlain, was created Earl of Worcester.

The court would return to Lambeth on a number of other occasions throughout Henry's reign, including in 1519 and 1520. Under Warham's successor, Thomas Cranmer, the palace buildings were extended and improved, and became central to the English Reformation. One can just imagine the discussions and debates that took place within its walls.

Visitor Information

Lambeth Palace is located on the south bank of the River Thames. If travelling via the tube or train, the nearest stations are Westminster, Waterloo, Vauxhall and Lambeth North. If the weather is pleasant, I recommend alighting at Westminster Station and making your way on foot, past Big Ben and the Palace of Westminster, towards Lambeth Bridge. Just across the bridge and on your left, you will see Morton's Tower. Wait here for your guided tour to begin. Remember this needs to be booked in advance, and keep in mind that tours are limited and booked on a first come, first served basis, so get your tickets early to avoid disappointment. To book tickets visit: www.archbishopofcanterbury.org/pages/guided-tours-.html

After your 90-minute tour, I highly recommend a visit to the Garden Museum (see entry for Garden Museum) housed in the restored medieval and Victorian church of St Mary's, situated only a few paces from Lambeth Palace. The church once contained the Howard Chapel, where several members of this prominent family were laid to rest, including Elizabeth Boleyn, mother of Mary, Anne and George Boleyn. At the time of writing, the museum was closed for restoration and expected to reopen in early 2017. Check the Garden Museum's website for more information: www.gardenmuseum.org.uk/

While in the area, note that roughly where the Novotel London Waterloo stands today, once stood Norfolk House, the palatial residence of the Dukes of Norfolk, where Catherine Howard spent time in the care of her step-grandmother, Agnes Tilney,

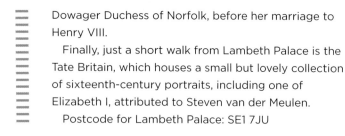

Dowager Duchess of Norfolk, before her marriage to Henry VIII.

Finally, just a short walk from Lambeth Palace is the Tate Britain, which houses a small but lovely collection of sixteenth-century portraits, including one of Elizabeth I, attributed to Steven van der Meulen.

Postcode for Lambeth Palace: SE1 7JU

You often boast to me that you have the king's ear and often have fun with him, freely and according to your whims. This is like having fun with tamed lions – often it is harmless, but just as often there is fear of harm. Often he roars in rage for no known reason, and suddenly the fun becomes fatal.

Thomas More

Situated in central London, Lincoln's Inn is one of the four ancient Inns of Court, where law students, barristers and Masters of the Bench (also known as 'Benchers'), have studied, worked and lived for almost 600 years. The tranquil and leafy 11-acre enclave, located within close proximity to the Westminster law courts, is an oasis of calm in the centre of the City, and is comprised of extensive gardens, and buildings from various periods of history, including Tudor.

The earliest documentary evidence for Lincoln's Inn dates to 1422, making it the oldest of any of the Inns of Court. It is, though, likely that its origins predate even these records, and that it evolved in the mid to latter part of the fourteenth century. However, it wasn't until the fifteenth century that Lincoln's Inn, along with Gray's Inn, the Middle Temple and the Inner Temple, began being referred to as the 'Inns of Court', denoting the fact that they provided accommodation and hospitality for their members – lawyers and law students – who appeared in the royal law courts. While the origin of the name Lincoln's Inn is not known for certain, it's thought to have derived from Thomas de Lincoln, a fourteenth-century Serjeant-at-Law (a senior practitioner who ranked above all other barristers).

During the Tudor period, the Inns of Court experienced a period of growth and prosperity, and by the end of Elizabeth's reign boasted an enrolment of around 1,000 members, becoming collectively known as 'the third University of England'. Not all those who enrolled planned to pursue a career in law, some simply viewed it as an opportunity to gain a general understanding of the common law (something not taught at either Oxford or Cambridge), while networking, and taking advantage of the unique intellectual and cultural opportunities such institutions offered.

The inns became popular with young men of noble birth and the sons of the gentry, who were eager to acquire skills in researching, writing and debating, along with some basic training in the use of arms. Members were also exposed to the latest fashions in music and dancing, and even gained experience in staging a variety of entertainments, including masques and plays.

In February 1496, Lincoln's Inn admitted one of its most famous members, an 18-year-old youth by the name of Thomas More.

A Snapshot of the Life of Thomas More

Thomas More was born in London on 7 February 1478, the son of John More, a bencher of Lincoln's Inn, and Agnes Graunger. Between 1485 and 1490, he attended St Anthony's School on Threadneedle Street, London, before spending two years as a page in the household of John Morton, Archbishop of Canterbury. The cardinal who, legend has it, was so impressed with his young charge, would often remark, 'This child here waiting at the table ... will prove a marvellous man'.

Between the ages of 14 and 16, More studied at Canterbury College, Oxford, mastering, among other subjects, Greek and Latin, before training as a law student at New Inn. In 1496, he was admitted to Lincoln's Inn, and called to the Bar in around 1501. While pursuing his legal career, More spent time at Charterhouse, the Carthusian monastery adjoining the inn, dedicating a number of years to both study and prayer. The monastic life certainly called to him, however, in the end, he chose instead to marry.

For the next decade, More's association with the inn continued, and he was appointed to a number of significant roles and positions, including being elected as both Autumn and Lent Reader, one of the highest honours that could be conferred on any member.

The year 1516 saw the publication of More's most important work, *Utopia*, and in the following year he entered the king's service, where he remained for the next fifteen years. During this time, he would become one of Henry VIII's most trusted civil servants and friends, serving as Lord Chancellor of England from 1529 to 1532. Unfortunately, this was not enough to save his head. In May 1532, More resigned as Lord Chancellor on the grounds of ill health. The following year he refused to attend Anne Boleyn's coronation, a blatant and very public act of defiance, which the king could not ignore. In 1534, More refused to swear the Oath of Supremacy, and so was arrested and imprisoned in the Tower of London.

Though the king was just a boy when he first met More, who went on to enjoy many years of royal favour, the erudite lawyer was executed for treason on 6 July 1535. He is said to have joked with the lieutenant who escorted him to the scaffold, 'see me safe up ... and for my coming down let me shift for myself'.

Four centuries later, he was canonised by Pope Pius XI.

Visitor Information

While many of Lincoln's Inn's buildings look Tudor, they are in fact of a much later date. There are, though, two buildings Thomas More would have known that have survived to this day, albeit in an altered state: the Old Hall and the Gatehouse.

The Old Hall was erected in around 1490, during the reign of the first Tudor monarch, Henry VII. In this space, Thomas and his fellow students, barristers and

benchers would have taken their meals and discussed the goings on of the day. The hall also played host to a variety of entertainments, including the Christmas revels, which all members were required to attend. This was a time for feasting and drinking, and general merrymaking.

The Tudor Gatehouse (opposite 40 Chancery Lane) was the principal entrance to the Inn until the middle of the nineteenth century when the present main entrance from Lincoln's Inn Fields was constructed. It was built between 1517 and 1521 but largely rebuilt and restored in the twentieth century. Take especial note of the oak doors that date from 1564.

The 'New Hall', opened by Queen Victoria in October 1845, is home to a copy of Hans Holbein's famous portrait of Thomas More as Lord Chancellor but even more precious is a miniature of More by Holbein that's displayed in the Council Room, alongside a document which bears his signature. Finally, the present library, built at around the same time as the Victorian hall, is home to many treasures, including a splendid first edition copy of More's *Utopia*, published in Louvain in 1516.

The precincts of the Inn are open to the public Monday to Friday, between 7 a.m. and 7 p.m. The Inn's buildings, however, can only be visited as part of a guided tour, with the exception of the seventeenth-century chapel, which is open on weekdays, between the hours of 9 a.m. and 5 p.m. Tours can be organised

Illustration of the sixteenth-century gateway, Lincoln's Inn, by E.W. Haslehust. (Copyright Bruce Hunt, maps.thehunthouse.com)

by emailing the address found on the Inn's website, under 'Tours and Visits', however, please note that Lincoln's Inn is currently undergoing major works, which means tours cannot be accommodated until after January 2018. Visit their website for more information: www.lincolnsinn.org.uk

It's also worth noting that members of the public can arrange a tour of the Elizabethan hall at Middle Temple, where the first performance of William Shakespeare's *Twelfth Night* is said to have taken place, with Queen Elizabeth herself the guest of honour. It's also possible to combine your tour with a buffet lunch, served in the spectacular Great Hall. For more information or to enquire about booking a tour, visit www.middletemplehall.org.uk

You might like to do as the author did and book a walking tour of the Inns of Court that includes a brief visit to all four of the medieval inns (exterior only). This is a great way to familiarise yourself with the history of these ancient societies, and learn about the colourful characters of legal London's past. I highly recommend the 2-hour tour run by London Walking Tours, which begins on Chancery Lane and ends outside Temple Church, one of London's oldest churches dating from the twelfth century.

London Walking Tours can be booked via their website www.london-walking-tours.co.uk/inns-of-court-tour.htm

Nearest underground station: Holborn or Chancery Lane

Lincoln's Inn postcode: WC2A 3TL

Staple Inn, 2016. Situated on High Holborn Street, close to Chancery Lane Station, Staple Inn was one of Tudor London's Inns of Chancery. It was originally attached to Gray's Inn, one of the four Inns of Court. (Author's collection)

... the plague reiynese in dyvers partes about London But thankes be god – Hackeney was never clerer than it is at this present.

Ralph Sadleir to Thomas Cromwell,
3 October 1537

In the heart of Hackney stands a little-known Tudor gem called Sutton House. It was built for the courtier and diplomat, Sir Ralph Sadleir (or Sadler), in around 1535, and is said to be the oldest home in East London. As a protégé of Thomas Cromwell's, Sadleir rose in influence and prospered during his mentor's ascendancy. However, unlike Cromwell, who was executed as a traitor and heretic in 1540, after Henry VIII's death Sadleir went on to serve Edward VI and Elizabeth I, and live until his eightieth year.

Over the centuries, Sutton House, or 'bryk place' as it was originally known, has housed a variety of occupants, including wealthy wool and silk merchants, Huguenot families and twentieth-century squatters, before being acquired by the National Trust in 1938, and finally opened to the public in 1994.

Tudor Hackney

Situated on the edge of the walled City, and less than 3 miles from Bishopsgate, Tudor Hackney was made up of three parishes: Hackney, Stoke Newington and Shoreditch. Unlike the

Sutton House, Hackney, 2016.
(Author's collection)

crowded and unwholesome streets of the nearby City, Hackney, with its open fields and pastureland, became a popular location for wealthy Londoners to build their country retreats. The 'healthful air' attracted the likes of Thomas Cromwell, Margaret Douglas, Countess of Lennox, Lucy Somerset, Baroness Latimer, and Henry Percy, 6th Earl of Northumberland.

The latter, who in the early 1520s had been romantically linked with Anne Boleyn, owned a house in Clapton, not far from where Sadleir would eventually build his brick mansion. In 1535, Henry VIII acquired this house from Percy, and it became known as 'the King's Place' (and later Brooke House). The king granted the house to Thomas Cromwell later that year, who appears to have largely rebuilt it. Clearly Hackney was seen to have restorative powers because in May 1537, an ailing Percy wrote to Cromwell asking him 'to helpe me to the kings hous of hakency whereby I trust the sonner to recover my helth'. Unfortunately, the country air did nothing to improve the earl's weak constitution, and he died there in June 1537.

Even so, its reputation as a place for rejuvenation continued well into the following century. Samuel Pepys recorded multiple visits to Hackney to 'take the ayre' in his seventeenth-century London diary, and in 1720, the historian John Strype described Hackney as a 'pleasant and healthful town, where divers nobles in former times had their country seats ...'.

Sutton House in the Sixteenth Century

At around the same time as Cromwell was rebuilding nearby King's Place, construction began on Sadleir's red-brick house, which stood on 'Hamerton Streete' in the hamlet of Homberton (Homerton), to the east of the Parish Church of St Augustine. The fact that it was known as 'bryk place' is indicative of how rare brick houses were in Hackney at the time, then just a quiet, rural village.

Sadleir built a three-storey 'H'-plan house, with a four-gabled frontage, decorated with the fashionable diaper patterning. It comprised two wings separated by a central range, with two cellars accessible from the outside. On the ground floor, the central block contained the Great Hall, paved with red tiles, and flanked by a service wing to the east and a parlour, lined with linenfold panelling, in the west. The first floor contained the panelled Great Chamber directly above the Great Hall, and a bedchamber with its own garderobe. The third floor housed the servants and children.

Many of the rooms boasted carved stone fireplaces, and the windows were made of oak with vertical mullions. This was a luxurious house indeed – a reflection of its owner's growing wealth and influence.

In 1540, Sadleir was knighted and appointed one of the king's two principal secretaries of state. By this time, his Hackney estate, of around 30 acres, consisted of multiple houses and outbuildings, a dovecote and extensive gardens. To the west of 'bryk place' stood another house, formerly the tannery, occupied at the time by Sadleir's father, Henry.

In 1550, he sold the majority of the estate to John Machell, a wealthy wool merchant who later became Sheriff of London. 'Bryk place' remained in the hands of the Machells for the remainder of the sixteenth century.

It wasn't until the twentieth century that Sadleir's former house acquired its current name, as a result of a widely held but erroneous belief that Thomas Sutton had lived there. In fact, Sutton, the very wealthy founder of Charterhouse Hospital and School, had lived in the old tannery, formerly occupied by Sadleir's father. The house was demolished in the early nineteenth century, to make way for a row of Georgian terraces, known as Sutton Place.

Sutton House Today

The house that greets visitors today has been greatly altered over the centuries, to serve a range of purposes. In the seventeenth century, it was home to a girls' school, one of several in the village of Hackney at the time. In the middle of the eighteenth century, the house was divided into two self-contained residences and leased out. A boys' school occupied part of the house in the early nineteenth century, and by 1895 the two parts of the house had been reunited and the premises became known as St John's Church Institute, a recreational club for men.

Today, the house is cared for by the National Trust and opened to the public. While much of the house Sadleir built has been lost or altered, there are some wonderful Tudor treasures left to see, namely in the Linenfold Parlour, the Little Chamber, the Great Chamber and Tudor Kitchen.

The first room you enter is the Linenfold Parlour. Its finely panelled walls and carved stone fireplace hark back to its Tudor origins, and provide a sense of how grand and impressive the original house would have been. There's an ineffable sense of timelessness in this room, as though at any moment its Tudor inhabitants might come striding through. It's not difficult to imagine Sadleir conducting business here, or sitting by the fire, quietly discussing the goings-on of Henry's court. At the time of writing, this room also housed a wonderful model of the sixteenth-century house.

Continue down the stairs into the cellar, originally accessed from the outside of the house. This is where food, beer and wine would have been stored in Tudor times. The house's Tudor foundations are visible at this level, and the eagle-eyed among us may be able to spot traces of the past imprinted on the bricks. After visiting the house in 2009, author Hilary Mantel wrote in an article for *The Guardian*, 'it was when I saw the grass stalk, the dog's paw print, that I began to sense the spring of 1535, when Thomas More was still alive and pearls were still warm on the neck of Anne Boleyn.'

Carry these images with you as you wander upstairs. The Little Chamber, possibly used as a bedroom by Sadleir's wife, contains some exquisite sixteenth-century panelling and leads into the Great Chamber. In this beautiful and spacious room, we can imagine Sadleir entertaining important guests, and banqueting by candlelight, late into the night. Be sure to look behind the hinged panelling above the fireplace to see remnants of the original Tudor brickwork.

At the far end of the room, a doorway leads into the Victorian Study, the principal bedchamber in Tudor times. The still extant garderobe reminds us that this was once Sadleir's private inner sanctum.

Back on the ground floor, the Georgian Parlour is home to some Tudor graffiti and the chapel is housed in what was once another cellar. Do not miss the Tudor kitchen, a space that would have been bustling almost around the clock with servants catering for Sadleir's large family. He and his wife had nine children, seven of which survived infancy.

Finally, head out into the courtyard where the Tudor knot garden once stood and where you'll find a surviving Tudor window. The Wenlock Barn that now encloses the courtyard was constructed as a function room in 1904, on the site of the sixteenth-century gardens.

Visitor Information

Sutton House is situated about a 5 to 10-minute walk from Hackney Central Station, through St John's Churchyard Gardens (open fields in Tudor times). Detailed directions can be found on Sutton House's website, under the 'How to get here' tab'.

In Sadleir's day, the main settlement was centred on and around what is now Mare Street. As you make your way towards St John's Churchyard Gardens, you will pass the fourteenth-century tower, which is now all that remains of St Augustine's, the medieval parish church of Hackney. When the present church of St John-at-Hackney replaced the parish church in the 1790s, a number of important Tudor monuments were moved to St John's, including memorials to Sir Christopher Urswick, rector of Hackney and confessor to Margaret Beaufort, and Lucy Somerset, Baroness Latimer, who served as a lady-in-waiting to Katherine Parr. These can still be seen in the church today.

Pause for a moment in the former churchyard; somewhere beneath the ground are interred the remains of Henry Percy, 6th Earl of Northumberland. He was almost certainly buried inside the body of the church, where the nobility were laid to rest, with a monument marking his grave, now, sadly, lost to time. While standing near his physical remains, you might find yourself pondering how very differently things might have turned out, had his romance with Anne Boleyn been allowed to flourish.

For directions, opening hours and other visitor information, visit Sutton House's website at: www.nationaltrust.org.uk/sutton-house-and-breakers-yard

Postcode: E9 6JQ

Every part of the Tower of London is pregnant with history and tradition.

Lord Ronald Sutherland Gower, 1901

No Tudor pilgrimage is complete without a visit to the world-famous Tower of London. Begun in the reign of William the Conqueror and largely completed in the reign of Edward I, this ancient fortress has stood sentinel over the City of London for more than 900 years. Throughout its long and often tumultuous history, it has served a range of purposes; namely those of fortress, royal palace, prison and execution site, however, it's also been home to an arsenal, royal mint, jewel house and menagerie.

Today it remains one of the city's most prominent and popular landmarks, welcoming well over 2 million visitors yearly, all eager to see the iconic Yeoman Warders, popularly known as 'Beefeaters', the ravens – legendary guardians of the Tower – and the dazzling Crown Jewels, which have been on public display since the seventeenth century. The Tower's darker side, which includes tales of royal disappearances and murders, torture, botched executions and countless ghosts, also draw in the crowds.

For those of us in search of remnants of the Tower's Tudor past, there is much to see, as we shall shortly explore. Each of the Tudor monarchs rode in procession from the Tower to Westminster for their coronations, and many prominent personalities of the day, including Thomas More, Anne Boleyn, George Boleyn, Thomas Cromwell, Catherine Howard, Thomas Seymour and Lady Jane Grey, spent their final hours within its shadow, before facing execution within the Tower itself, or on Tower Hill. Their mortal remains were later unceremoniously buried in the Chapel of St Peter ad Vincula, where they remain to this day.

ENTRY TO THE TRAITORS GATE

'To see it [the Tower]', said the sculptor and writer Lord Ronald Sutherland Gower, 'is to conjure up a vision of scenes, some brilliant and stately, some tragic and awful, but all full of deepest interest ...', an apt description for a place of such intriguing contrasts, and one that has witnessed the gamut of human emotions, from elation to utter despair. Let us now explore some of these 'scenes'.

The Tudor Highlights

St Thomas's Tower, built by Edward I between 1275 and 1279 to supplement the Tower's royal accommodation, is one of a group of buildings known today as the Medieval Palace.

The Tower of London viewed from the
south, 2016. (Author's collection)

The water gate, built at the same time, provided a new river
entrance to the Tower, and is today known as Traitor's Gate
because of the many prisoners accused of treason who are
said to have passed under it.

The buildings that make up the Medieval Palace were
refurbished in 1532 in preparation for Anne Boleyn's coronation,
which took place in the summer of 1533. St Thomas's Tower was
restored to provide accommodation for William Sandys and John
de Vere, the 15th Earl of Oxford, Henry VIII's Lord Chamberlain
and Lord Great Chamberlain respectively, who were in charge
of organising the lavish coronation ceremonies. If you look up,
it's still possible to see the enormous beams installed by Henry's
master carpenter, James Nedeham, to fortify the roof in order
to withstand the weight of the ceremonial guns that would be
fired to mark Anne's arrival at the Tower. The Tudor chronicler
Edward Hall furnishes us with the details:

On Thursday 29 May, Lady Anne, marquess of Pembroke,
was received as queen of England by all the lords of
England. And the mayor and aldermen, with all the guilds
of the City of London, went to Greenwich in their barges
after the best fashion, with also a barge of bachelors of
the mayor's guild richly hung with cloth of gold with a
great number to wait on her. And so all the lords with the
mayor and all the guilds of London brought her by water
from Greenwich to the Tower of London, and there the
king's grace received her as she landed, and then over a
thousand guns were fired at the Tower, and others were
fired at Limehouse, and on other ships lying in the Thames.

Over 1,000 cannons, hence the need for the sturdy roof!

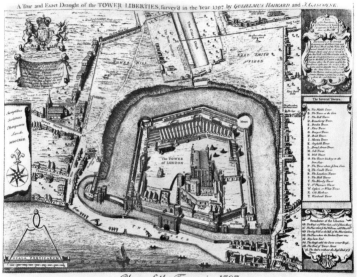

Plan of the Tower in 1597
by Haiward and Gascoyne.

A plan of the Tower of London in 1597, by Gulielmus Haiward and
J. Gascoyne. (Author's collection)

On the south wall walk, pause about halfway between the
Wakefield Tower and the Lanthorn Tower, reconstructed in
the late nineteenth century after being destroyed by fire. Turn
away from the iconic nineteenth-century Tower Bridge and look
towards the open grass area in front of the White Tower. This
space, as depicted on the information board, once contained
many buildings, including the King's Great Hall, where Anne and
George Boleyn were tried separately on 15 May 1536, and the
Queen's Lodgings, a lavish suite of rooms custom built for Anne.
In these new sumptuous apartments, Anne would spend the
two nights prior to her coronation in joyful celebration, secure
in her position by Henry's side, and with a royal baby in her belly.

In a tragic twist of fate, these same rooms would bear
witness to her imprisonment, from Tuesday, 2 May to Friday,

19 May 1536. In these, her darkest and final days, she must have thought back to those happier times and wondered how and why it all went so terribly wrong.

Less than six years later, in February 1542, Anne's young cousin, Catherine Howard, would spend her last wretched days in the same beautiful apartments. According to Eustace Chapuys, Catherine requested that the block be brought to her 'that she might know how to place herself'. Unlike her cousin and predecessor who'd been beheaded with a sword, Catherine was to face the executioner's axe – a cruel and brutal end for Henry's once beloved 'rose without a thorn'.

When exiting the Lanthorn Tower, look out toward the river. The building that stands virtually opposite is the Cradle Tower, from where prisoners John Gerard and John Arden managed to escape in 1599. It is open to the public and can be accessed via Water Lane.

As already mentioned, the Tower was used as a prison in the sixteenth century, and many of those incarcerated left behind some marvellous graffiti. In the Salt Tower, look out for an intricate astrological sphere carved by Hew Draper, an innkeeper from Bristol accused of sorcery, and in the Broad Arrow Tower, keep an eye out for a carving believed to have been made by Giovanni Battista Castiglione, Princess Elizabeth's Italian tutor, who was imprisoned by Mary I in 1556.

Straight ahead of you as you enter the Martin Tower is a carving that reads 'boullen', traditionally said to have been left by George Boleyn, who may have been imprisoned here. Continuing along the north wall walk, the Brick Tower is home to a 'Royal Beasts' exhibition about the wild and exotic animals that were kept at the Tower from the twelfth to the nineteenth century. In 1598, a German lawyer by the name of Paul Hentzner visited the Tower and saw the royal menagerie:

> On coming out of the Tower, we were led to a small house close by, where are kept variety of creatures, viz. – three lionesses; one lion of great size, called Edward VI. From his having been born in that reign: a tiger; a lynx;

a wolf excessively old – this is a very scarce animal in England, so that their sheep and cattle stray about in great numbers, free from any danger, though without anybody to keep them; there is, besides, a porcupine, and an eagle. All these creatures are kept in a remote place, fitted up for the purpose with wooden lattices, at the Queen's expense.

The Bowyer Tower is where, according to legend, George, Duke of Clarence, brother of Edward IV and Richard III, was imprisoned in 1477 and eventually died. The circumstances of George's death are shrouded in mystery. Some sources say he was secretly beheaded, others suggest he was killed by his younger brother, Richard, but the most popular story is that he was drowned in a barrel of malmsey (sweet wine imported from Greece), a legend perpetuated by William Shakespeare in his play *Richard III*. While it may sound like pure fiction, a portrait housed in the National Portrait Gallery may offer some supporting evidence.

The portrait depicts an unknown noblewoman, who, around her right wrist, wears a bracelet with a small barrel charm. Why is this significant? Because the sitter is believed to be Margaret Pole, Countess of Salisbury, daughter of George, Duke of Clarence and Isabel Neville. Is this then an allusion to her father's unconventional death? While certainly interesting, it does not provide conclusive evidence because the identity of the sitter is not certain.

Like her father, the Countess of Salisbury, who'd been a close companion of Katherine of Aragon, met a truly grisly end. On the morning of 27 May 1541, after having spent two long years imprisoned as a traitor at the Tower, 67-year-old Margaret was beheaded in a private execution, by an inexperienced headsman. The pitiful and cruel death sent shock waves through the Tudor court. If Henry VIII could order the death of a frail old lady, his eldest daughter's own godmother, and feel no remorse then surely no one was safe. She is buried in the Chapel of St Peter ad Vincula, alongside many other Tudors, including bishops, queens and dukes.

The first-floor cell of the Beauchamp Tower is home to a sea of Tudor graffiti including a carving of what appears to be Anne Boleyn's falcon badge, minus its crown and sceptre. The majestic bird stands bare, stripped of its royal regalia, like its mistress stood in the dying days of spring 1536. It's possible that this poignant symbol was etched by one of the men arrested alongside Anne, as the Beauchamp Tower was the perfect place to house high-ranking prisoners, on account of its ample accommodation and proximity to the Lieutenant's Lodgings, home to the Constable of the Tower or his deputy. These buildings once stood on the site of the present-day Queen's House.

Nearby, the name 'Jane' is roughly carved into the stonework, perhaps the work of Lady Jane Grey's husband, Guildford Dudley, who was imprisoned at the Tower in 1553–54, along with his father and brothers. A striking and beautiful memorial to the Dudley family can be found to the right of the fireplace, their family crest intricately carved into the wall.

The Bloody Tower's name is based on one of the greatest mysteries of the Tower of London, the disappearance and alleged murder of the sons of Edward IV, popularly known as the Princes in the Tower. It was during the Tudor reign that the building, originally known as the Garden Tower, acquired its more sinister name because it was believed to have been where Edward's two cherubic blonde boys had their lives snuffed out.

After the death of their father, 12-year-old Edward V and his 9-year-old brother Richard of Shrewsbury, Duke of York, were living at the Tower under the protection of their uncle, Richard,, Duke of Gloucester, while preparations were underway for young Edward's coronation. As it turned out, Edward was never crowned and on 6 July 1483, his uncle Richard was crowned instead.

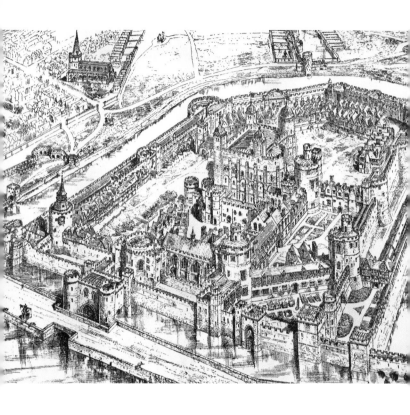

The princes remained lodged at the Tower for a short time before simply disappearing. Many, including Sir Thomas More, believed that Richard III had ordered the death of his nephews, however, it has never been conclusively proven. In 1674, the bones of two children were found buried near the White Tower and reinterred in Westminster Abbey as the remains of the princes, but they have never been forensically tested leaving their identity open to speculation.

Like the Beauchamp Tower, the Bloody Tower was also used to house high-ranking prisoners, including Thomas Cranmer, who was imprisoned there before being taken to Oxford, where he was burnt at the stake in 1556. Today, the tower is furnished

Reconstruction of the Tower of London, as it would have appeared in the sixteenth century, by H.W. Brewer. All Hallows Church can be seen in the top left corner, next to the site of the scaffold on Tower Hill. (Author's collection)

as it may have appeared during the extended imprisonment of Sir Walter Raleigh, charged with treason for his involvement in a conspiracy against James I.

The imposing White Tower, begun during the reign of William the Conqueror, is the oldest medieval building at the Tower of London and has much to offer the Tudor enthusiast, including a wonderful exhibition from the collection of the Royal Armouries. Some of the highlights include armour made for Henry VIII in 1515, beautifully engraved with the entwined initials of Henry and Katherine of Aragon, Tudor roses and pomegranates. Henry was around 24-years-old at the time and judging by the size of the armour, which measures 106cm around the chest and 88cm at the waist, was in fine physical shape. Compare this to Henry VIII's field and tournament armour made in Greenwich in 1540. The then 49-year-old ailing king required armour that measured 138cm around the chest and 129½cm at the waist – a far cry from his former athletic self!

On 7 July 1600, Baron Waldstein visited the Tower and was taken on a tour of the armoury, later describing it in his diary:

The Armoury in the Tower is particularly interesting, with a fine collection of cannon, pikes, shields, missiles, arrows, cross-bows, javelins and other weapons.

First of all, downstairs, we were shown some twenty siege guns mounted on gun carriages, and here we saw those iron devices which they fire from naval guns to destroy ships' rigging, for these English guns are most commonly used in battles at sea. Nearby we were shown a place which had 16 cases or containers full of great iron pikes ... There were arrows which can be loaded into guns, and – just the reverse – bows which can shoot leaden bullets ... We then visited another armoury full of spears decorated with silk and gold, belonging to the Royal Guard.

Paul Hentzner, in 1598, also saw the 'body armour of Henry VIII' and the 'lance of Charles Brandon, Duke of Suffolk, three spans thick'.

Before leaving the White Tower be sure to visit the Norman Chapel of St John the Evangelist – a beautiful and rare survival.

The Scaffold Site and Chapel Royal of St Peter ad Vincula

In front of the Chapel of St Peter ad Vincula stands an evocative circular memorial to the people who were executed inside the Tower, including five Tudor women all beheaded for treason: Anne Boleyn (1536), Margaret Pole (1541), Catherine Howard (1542), Jane Boleyn (1542) and Lady Jane Grey (1554). Designed by Brian Catling and unveiled in 2006, the memorial bears the names of those executed and a beautiful poem:

Gentle visitor pause a while, where you stand death cut away the light of many days. Here jewelled names were broken from the vivid thread of life. May they rest in peace while we walk the generations around their strife and courage under these restless skies.

A touching tribute. However, it does not mark the site of the original scaffold, which stood on the north side of the White Tower, close to the entrance of the Waterloo Barracks and

Crown Jewels Exhibition. Baron Waldstein noted four scaffolds in this area on his visit:

> Visited the castle by the Thames: it is usually called the Tower of London. It is defended with several moats, encircled by triple walls, and inside it is so full of houses that it gives visitors the impression of a town. A large open space in front of the Tower [the White Tower] contains four scaffolds, and here a number of dukes, earls, and others have been executed for treason.

Stand facing the White Tower, with your back to the Waterloo Barracks and there before you, virtually unchanged, is the last thing those condemned to die within the Tower saw.

It's natural to now want to visit the final resting place of the people that perished here, all of whom are buried in the Chapel Royal of St Peter ad Vincula, alongside many of those who met their end in public executions on Tower Hill. While Anne and George Boleyn, Lady Rochford, Catherine Howard and Margaret Pole were buried in the church's chancel, others including Norris, Weston, Brereton and Smeaton – the men charged alongside Anne Boleyn – were laid to rest in the adjacent churchyard, where the Waterloo Block now stands.

Join a Yeoman Warder's tour to access the chapel or visit in the last hour of normal opening time, when the public is permitted access. This is a moving and contemplative way in which to end your visit to the Tower.

As you make your way to the main exit, take note of the Bell Tower (not currently open to the public), where Thomas More and the poet Thomas Wyatt were once imprisoned, and later in the century, Princess Elizabeth too. According to tradition, Wyatt witnessed the execution of his friends – Boleyn, Norris, Weston, Brereton and Smeaton – from his prison cell, inspiring him to write the poem, '*Innocentia Veritas Viat Fides Circumdederunt me intimici me*', reflecting on the precarious nature of court life and the reversal of fortune so often experienced by those closest to the king. He ends

each verse with a Latin phrase that can be translated as, 'Thunder rolls around the throne'. Verse three and four are particularly moving:

> These bloody days have broken my heart.
> My lust, my youth did them depart,
> And blind desire of estate.
> Who hastes to climb seeks to revert.
> Of truth, circa Regna tonat.

> The Bell Tower showed me such sight
> That in my head sticks day and night.
> There did I lean out of a grate,
> For all favour, glory, or might,
> That yet circa Regna tonat.

Early twentieth-century photo of
the interior of the Chapel of St
Peter ad Vincula, Tower of London.
Among those buried in the chapel
are Thomas More, Anne Boleyn,
George Boleyn, Thomas Cromwell,
Catherine Howard and Lady Jane Grey.
(Author's collection)

Outside the Tower precinct are two points of Tudor interest. The first is the Queen's Stairs, found opposite the drawbridge that leads to the Byward Postern Gate. This is one of three riverside entrances to the Tower, and one often used by royalty in the sixteenth century. It's here that we can imagine the Tudor kings and queens arriving in all their finery.

The second is the site of the scaffold on Tower Hill, in what is now Trinity Square Gardens, where around 125 people died in public executions. These grisly affairs drew in large crowds of spectators, often accommodated in special viewing galleries erected around the scaffold.

As Lord Ronald Sutherland Gower said, 'Every part of the Tower of London is pregnant with history and tradition', pregnant with the memories of those cataclysmic events that seem to linger and envelope you as you walk its ancient historic grounds.

Visitor Information

While the nearest underground station is Tower Hill, a 5-minute walk from the main entrance, visitors might like to do as the author enjoys and alight at London Bridge Station on the south side of the Thames.

Byward Postern Gate, Tower of
London, 2016. (Author's collection)

Site of the scaffold on Tower Hill,
c. 1900. (Author's collection)

Site of the scaffold on Tower Hill, 2013. On or near this spot, around 125 people died in public executions, including many notable Tudors. (Author's collection)

From there it's a leisurely 15-minute walk along the south bank of the river, which affords some wonderful views of the Tower, across Tower Bridge and to the main entrance.

I highly recommend pre-booking your tickets online to avoid the long queues at the ticket office. Even better, become a member of the Historic Royal Palaces and enjoy free access to all six palaces in their care, including Hampton Court and the Tower of London, while also helping to preserve these historic gems for future generations. The annual membership includes some other additional benefits, including a 10 per cent discount in the restaurants, shops and cafés at their venues, which is fantastic, especially if you plan to buy lots of Tudor trinkets at the gift stores! To find out more, visit www.hrp.org.uk/support-us/individuals/membership

The brave among us might like to consider joining one of the Tower's Twilight Tours, which allow you unique after-hours access, or perhaps you'd like to be a part of the Ceremony of the Keys? This ancient tradition of locking up the Tower at night has taken place each evening for at least the last 700 years! This is a very popular ceremony and while it is free, needs to be booked well in advance. Find out more at www.hrp.org.uk/tower-of-london/whats-on

Just a stone's throw from the Tower is All Hallows by the Tower, the oldest church in the City of London (see separate entry for All Hallows by the Tower), where the bodies of some of those executed on Tower Hill were held temporarily, before being buried.

The Tower of London is managed by the Historic Royal Palaces.

For detailed visitor information, visit their website at www.hrp.org.uk/tower-of-london

Postcode: EC3N 4AB

The Kings Grace [Henry VII], intending to amplify and increase the royalty of this noble and solemn feast with many divers and goodly acts of pleasure, let cause Westminster Hall – the which is of great length, breadth, largeness, and right crafty building – his walls to be richly hanged with pleasant cloth of Arras ...

From *The Receyt of the Ladie Kateryne,* an account of Katherine of Aragon's arrival to England, her entry into London and marriage to Arthur Tudor

Between 1097 and 1099 a grand new hall was built at the Palace of Westminster for King William II. The vast building measured 73m by 20m and covered an area of around 1,547 square metres, making it by far the largest hall in England at the time, and probably in Europe too. The hall was enclosed by 2m-thick stone walls – the inner faces of which were plastered and painted – and contained an arcade with large arches, which ran all the way around the hall, from where banners were hung on special occasions.

Three hundred years later, during the reign of King Richard II, it was virtually rebuilt. The task of remodelling the hall was assigned to Henry Yevele, the king's chief mason, and Hugh Herland, a talented master carpenter. The pair had worked together on the construction of the Jewel Tower, and would now collaborate once again on this important royal commission. Yevele heightened the walls, inserted new windows and added a porch and two flanking towers to the north end, while Herland replaced the old roof with a magnificent hammer-beam roof decorated with twenty-six carved angels, which survives to this day.

Trials and Banquets

For 700 years, Westminster Hall was at the very centre of the English legal system. By the middle of the thirteenth century, the government finance office, known as the Exchequer, was housed in a building adjoining the Great Hall, but in the hall itself sat the Common Pleas, King's Bench and Chancery.

During the Tudor reign, the hall was the setting for many important state trials, including those of Sir Thomas More and John Fisher in 1535, and Sir Henry Norris, Sir Francis Weston, William Brereton and Mark Smeaton in 1536. The latter four men had been arrested alongside Queen Anne Boleyn and her brother, George, and accused of adultery with the queen. Unfortunately for the defendants, it was virtually impossible to be acquitted of treason in Tudor times, especially in the aforementioned cases where the king's wishes were well known. Furthermore, the accused was required to defend him or herself, and prove that they were innocent of the charges laid against them in the indictment. A challenging task when you consider that they were only made aware of the specific charges at the trial.

However, in July 1534, a remarkable event occurred, Lord Dacre was unanimously acquitted of high treason. As the imperial ambassador, Eustace Chapuys noted in his letter to Charles V, this was a highly unusual occurrence:

> ... he [Lord Dacre] was declared innocent by 24 lords, unanimously, and acquitted by 12 judges according to the custom of England; which is one of the most novel things that have been heard of for 100 years, for no one ever knew a man come to the point he had done and escape.

Lord Dacre had been lucky. Trials of high treason usually ended with the convicted being sentenced to be hung, drawn and quartered, a barbarous punishment that the monarch could commute to beheading. This is in fact what happened in all the cases mentioned above.

State trials aside, the hall also provided a magnificent setting for royal feasts and lavish coronation banquets. On 14 November 1501, Prince Arthur Tudor married Katherine of Aragon at old St Paul's Cathedral. What followed was almost two weeks of celebrations and festivities, which included banquets, jousts and disguisings, the details of which are recorded in *The Receyt of the Ladie Kateryne*, a contemporary account of, among other things, Katherine's arrival to England, her entry into London and marriage to Prince Arthur. In Gordon Kipling's introduction to the *Receyt*, he defines disguisings as:

> a collaboration between a 'master of the revels', who superintended the construction of the costumes and pageants, and the personnel of the Chapel Royal, who probably devised them and certainly acted in them … As a consequence, the Tudor disguising consisted of a two-part performance: an elaborate and spectacular prologue preceded a costumed dance.

The author of the *Receyt* records one such disguising as taking place at Westminster Hall on the evening of Friday, 19 November, five days after Katherine and Arthur's marriage. The hall had been hung with splendid tapestries and a cupboard, seven shelves high, erected to display the king's glittering plate. Once Henry VII and Elizabeth of York had taken their seats under their cloths of estate, at the upper end of the hall, there entered the first of a series of pageants from the lower end, 'a castle right and cunningly devised, set upon certain wheels and drawn into the said hall by four great beasts with chains of gold'. This was an important moment in the history of English courtly entertainment because it was the first time that pageant cars on wheels had been used.

The king and queen, illumined by torchlight and surrounded by their family and noble guests, including the king's mother, Margaret Beaufort, the newlyweds, Prince Arthur and Princess Katherine, and Arthur's younger brother, Henry, watched as

Old St Paul's Cathedral by H.W. Brewer. (Author's collection)

from within the castle appeared eight ladies peering out of the windows. At each of the castle's four corners stood a turret and within each turret, a 'child apparelled like a maiden … singing full sweetly and harmoniously' as the castle crossed the length of the hall.

The second pageant was a ship, again set upon wheels, which travelled the length of the hall and stopped before the king, near to the castle. The author recorded what followed:

> The masters of the ship and their company in their countenance, speeches, and demeanour used and behaved themselves after the manner and guise of mariners, and there cast their anchors somewhat beside the said castle. In the which ship there was a goodly and fair lady, in her apparel like unto the Princess of Spain. Out and from the said ship descended down by a ladder two weel-beseen and goodly persons calling themselves Hope and Desire, passing toward the aforementioned

> castle with their banners, in manner and form as
> ambassadors from [the] Knights of the Mount of Love
> unto the Ladies within the castle, making great instance
> in the behalf of the said knights for the intent to attain
> the favours of the said ladies present ...

However, the ladies refused, and so were warned that the knights would 'for this unkind refusal' attack the castle. We then hear of the third and final pageant, where eight knights roll into the hall on a mountain, and stop near the king:

> And there they took their standing upon the other side of
> the ship ... alighted from the said mount with their banners
> displayed and hastily sped them to the aforementioned
> castle, which they forthwith assaulted so and in such wise
> that the ladies, yielding themselves, descended from the
> said castle and submitted them to the power, grace and
> will of those noble knights being right freshly disguised,
> and the ladies also, four of them after the English fashion
> and the other four after the manner of Spain, danced
> together divers and many goodly dances. And in the
> time of her dancing the three pageants – the castle, the
> ship, and the mountain – removed and departed.

Dancing and a lavish banquet followed the disguising. Arthur danced with his aunt, Lady Cecily, and Katherine with one of her ladies. Lastly, Arthur's 10-year-old brother, Henry, descended from the dais and danced two bass dances with his sister, Margaret. The boy – who before the decade was out, would become England's new king and Katherine's second husband – threw caution to the wind and feeling encumbered by his layers of clothing, 'suddenly cast off his gown and danced in his jacket in so goodly and pleasant a manner that it was to the King and Queen right great and single pleasure'.

Coronation Banquets

Arthur Tudor died before he could succeed his father to the throne, and so his younger brother, Henry, took his place and his wife, and was crowned King Henry VIII on 24 June 1509, in a joint coronation ceremony that saw Katherine fulfil her lifelong dream of becoming England's queen. In keeping with tradition, the coronation was followed by a magnificent banquet at Westminster Hall, where newly crowned monarchs had been honoured for more than 300 years, and where they would continue to be so, until the nineteenth century.

This honour was not only reserved for kings, queens who were crowned separately from their husbands also enjoyed

King Henry VIII from Foxe's *Book of Martyrs*, 1563. The king is seated beneath a canopy of state in a beautifully adorned chamber, typical of Tudor royal palaces. (By kind permission of the Stationery Office)

a coronation feast. A notable example is that of Anne Boleyn, who was almost six months pregnant with the future Elizabeth I at the time of her coronation. After Henry VIII's second wife was crowned at Westminster Abbey on 1 June 1533, guests retreated to the hall for a sumptuous feast. The Tudor chronicler Edward Hall recalled that:

> ... when the mass was done they left, every man in his order, to Westminster Hall, she [Anne Boleyn] still going under the canopy, crowned, with two sceptres in her hands, my Lord Wiltshire her father, and Lord Talbot leading her, and so dined there; and there was made the most honourable feast that has been seen.

From the aforementioned account, and the *Letters and Papers, Foreign and Domestic, of the Reign of Henry VIII*, we know that the hall had been richly decorated for the occasion, the walls hung with splendid tapestries and expensive fabrics. At the hall's upper end, twelve steps led up to a dais, where the new queen dined at a great marble table, shared only with Thomas Cranmer, the Archbishop of Canterbury. To ensure the queen's comfort, the marble throne, where Anne would spend hours seated below a rich cloth of estate, was fitted with a comfortable inner chair, specifically designed for the pregnant queen. Below, her subjects sat in order of precedence, and feasted, depending on their rank, on up to three courses, each containing between twenty-four and thirty dishes! Meanwhile, the Duke of Suffolk, in his role as high steward, kept order from atop his horse trapped in crimson velvet, while Lord William Howard, also on horseback, helped officiate.

The king, along with the ambassadors of France and Venice, watched events unfold from the privacy of a 'little closet' that projected out from the east side of the hall, overlooking the dais. While the exact cost of this elaborate banquet is unknown, it must have been phenomenal. It was the huge cost associated with these events that eventually led to them being abandoned.

George IV's coronation banquet in 1821 was the last to be held in the hall. His successor, William IV, veered away from a tradition that he found exceedingly expensive. All subsequent monarchs followed suit, and so ended Westminster Hall's time as the venue for coronation banquets.

Westminster Hall Highlights

Most visitors to the hall today enter via the north door (the lower end), and as such are greeted with a breathtaking and uninterrupted view of the Great Hall. From this vantage point, you can truly savour the ingeniuity and magnificence of the hammer-beam roof, and marvel at the hall's mammoth proportions. Once you've caught your breath, turn your back to the upper end of the hall, and face the north door. The space beyond the doors was the site of one of the main courtyards of the medieval Palace of Westminster, New Palace Yard, where jousts were held, and where a large canopied fountain once stood. On important occasions, such as the coronation of a new monarch, the fountain flowed with wine.

To the right of the north door, on the hall's east wall, you will find a large doorway surmounted by a medieval carving of a man holding bags of money. This once led to the Receipt of the Exchequer, an office of the Exchequer responsible for the receipt and payment of money. As you walk towards the centre of the hall, pause for a moment below one of the twenty-six angels that form part of the roof. Note how each angel (minus the wings) has been painstakingly carved out of a solid oak beam. The angels each hold a shield carved with the arms of Richard II, the man responsible for remodelling the hall between 1394 and 1399.

No doubt your attention will also be drawn to the five statues in the window enclosures. These were part of thirteen stone statues, representing each of the kings from Edward the Confessor to Richard II, commissioned by the latter in the late fourteenth century. A further six statues can be seen in niches on the south wall. Originally, the robes would have been painted a vibrant red and green and each king would have worn a gilded crown.

As you make your way towards the upper end of the hall, look out for the display containing fragments of the King's High Table made of Purbeck marble, where, among others, Richard III, Henry VIII, Anne Boleyn and Elizabeth I dined during their coronation banquets. At the southern end of the hall, stop at the foot of the stairs and imagine the raised dais that once stood in its place, upon which countless English monarchs dined and presided over their coronation banquets.

Look up to your left, between the first and second windows from the right once projected the timber closet, or gallery, from where Henry VIII watched his wife's coronation celebrations. The gated stairs below lead to the Chapel of St Mary Undercroft, built by Edward I in 1297, and heavily restored in the nineteenth century after the fire of 1834 that destroyed much of the medieval palace. This was originally the lower storey of a two-storey chapel, dedicated to St Stephen, where the royal household worshipped. The upper chapel, completed in 1348 under King Edward III, was probably reserved for the royal family and their guests. Today, only the undercroft, or lower chapel, survives and is usually only open to Members of Parliament and their families, for weddings and christenings. St Stephen's Hall now occupies the site of the medieval upper chapel.

Finally, make your way to the top of the stairs, to St Stephen's Porch, constructed in the 1840s, and admire the view over the hall. Its sturdy walls have witnessed so much history, from the daily administration of a kingdom to elaborate court ceremonies and great state trials. How can one not be moved by such a place?

Visitor Information

To access Westminster Hall, overseas visitors must book a tour of the Houses of Parliament, which covers the House of Lords and House of Commons, and Westminster Hall. While UK residents can buy tickets for the public guided tours, they also have the option of arranging a tour through their local MP. These are free of charge but need to be booked well in advance, by contacting your local MP or a member of the House of Lords. Some specialist themed tours are also available. For further information, visit: www.parliament.uk/visiting/visiting-and-tours/tours-of-parliament

The UK Parliament website has a series of excellent videos which show what the hall would have looked like at two key moments in its history: 1099 and 1400. These video reconstructions can be accessed at the following link: www.parliament.uk/visiting/online-tours/virtualtours/westminster-hall-tours/tour-video

Furthermore, I highly recommend taking the online virtual tour of Westminster Hall, which allows you to explore the interior of the hall at your leisure: www.parliament.uk/visiting/online-tours/virtualtours/westminster-hall-tours

Postcode for the Houses of Parliament: SW1A 0AA

Part 3

Churches
& Religious
Houses

There has been a church on the site of All Hallows since the seventh century, when Erkenwald, the future Bishop of London, founded it as a chapel of Barking Abbey, a female Benedictine order which he'd established east of London. Due to this connection, the church is also known as 'All Hallows Barking' or 'Berkyngechirche'.

Before long, the early wooden structure was replaced by a stone church, which was enlarged and altered over the centuries. The church's tower was rebuilt in 1659, following a devastating fire, and, along with some sections of the church's outer walls, was all that survived the Blitz of 1940–41. Interestingly, it was from the top of the tower that Samuel Pepys watched the Great Fire consume London in 1666, noting in his diary for 5 September, 'I up to the top of Barkeing steeple, and there saw the saddest sight of desolation that I ever saw; everywhere great fires ... the fire being spread as far as I could see it'.

On account of All Hallows' proximity to the Tower of London, it has served in the past as a temporary burial place for those executed on Tower Hill, one of a number of places around London where public executions took place. In Stow's *A Survey of London*, he recorded the following:

> Upon this Hill [Tower Hill] is alwayes readily prepared at the charges of the cittie a large Scaffolde and Gallowes of Timber, for the execution of such Traytors or Transgressors, as are deliuered out of the Tower, or otherwise to the Shiriffes of London by writ there to be executed.

On 22 June 1535, John Fisher, Bishop of Rochester, was beheaded on Tower Hill for refusing to take the Oath of Succession and acknowledge Henry VIII as supreme head of the Church in England. Following his execution, his headless

body was buried 'in the churchyard of Barking by the north door', as recorded in the *Chronicle of the Grey Friars of London*, and his head displayed on London Bridge as a warning to other would-be traitors.

In *The Life and Death of That Renowned John Fisher Bishop of Rochester*, attributed to Richard Hall (*c*. 1535–1604) and edited and published by Thomas Bayly in 1655, a curious tale is told about the bishop's head that is worth reproducing in full:

> The next day after his burying, the head being parboyled, was pricked upon a pole and set on high upon London Bridge, among the rest of the holy Carthusians heads that suffered death lately before him. And here I cannot omit to declare unto you the miraculous sight of this head, which after it had stood up the space of fourteen

All Hallows by the Tower, 2016.
(Author's collection)

dayes upon the bridge, could not be perceived to wast nor consume, neither for the weather, which then was very hot, neither for the parboyling in hot water, but grew daily fresher and fresher, so that in his life-time he never looked so well, for his cheeks being beautified with a comely red, the face looked as though it had beholden the people passing by, and would have spoken to them, which many took for a miracle, that Almighty God was pleased to shew above the course of nature, in this preserving the fresh and lively colour in his face, surpassing the colour he had being alive, whereby was noted to the world the innocence and holinesse of this blessed Father, that thus innocently was content to lose his head in defence of his Mother, the holy Catholique Church of Christ; wherefore the people coming daily to see this strange sight, the passage over the bridge was so stopped with their going and coming, that almost neither cart nor horse could passe: and therfore at the end of fourteen daies this Executioner was commanded to throw downe the head in the night-time into the River of Thames, and in the place thereof was set the head of the most blessed and constant Martyr, Sir Thomas Moore, his Companion and fellow in all his troubles ...

Just two weeks after Fisher's execution, on 6 July 1535, as Henry VIII and Anne Boleyn prepared to set off from Windsor Castle on their annual summer progress, Sir Thomas More, the king's former friend and Lord Chancellor, was beheaded for the same offence as Bishop Fisher. More's body was then taken to All Hallows 'and then was tane [taken?] up the Bishop again and both of them buried within the Tower', in the Chapel of St Peter ad Vincula, where they remain to this day. Thomas More's head was also exhibited on London Bridge, a macabre practice that continued into the seventeenth century.

When visiting the church today, look out for three carved wooden statues that date from the late fifteenth and early sixteenth centuries, including one of St James of Compostela, and a winged triptych, known as the Tate Panel, from about 1500, which was once housed in a chantry chapel north of All Hallows and parallel to the main church.

The church is also home to seventeen memorial brasses that date from 1389 to 1651, and an elaborate sixteenth-century monument to Hieronimus Benalius, an Italian who lived in Seething Lane during the reign of Elizabeth I.

Keep an eye out for the oldest surviving Saxon arch in the City of London and be sure to visit the Crypt Museum, housed in part of the original Saxon church, which is home to treasures from the Roman occupation of the site, including a section of tessellated floor from a second-century house.

Visitor Information

All Hallows is located on Byward Street just a short walk away from the Tower of London and the site of the scaffold on Tower Hill. The nearest underground station is Tower Hill.

If you're in need of lunch or a fortifying beverage after walking in the footsteps of the many poor souls executed on Tower Hill, I recommend dropping into the nearby, and aptly named, Hung, Drawn & Quartered pub, where you'll find good food and ale, and the walls lined with portraits of famous people from history, including a number of Tudor monarchs. For more information or to book a table, go to www.hung-drawn-and-quartered.co.uk

For All Hallows opening times and other visitor information visit www.ahbtt.org.uk

Postcode: EC3R 5BJ

On the night of 16–17 April 1941, hundreds of German bombers attacked south and central London for almost eight hours, killing and maiming thousands of civilians. Among the buildings bombed that night were eighteen hospitals and thirteen churches, including Chelsea Old Church.

A parachute mine detonated nearby, destroying the majority of the church, which at the time consisted of a seventeenth-century tower and nave, a thirteenth-century chancel and two adjoining fourteenth-century chapels.

These chapels were private property, the one in the north, now known as the Lawrence Chapel, was built for the lord of the manor of Chelsea. The chapel in the south, known as More's Chapel, was rebuilt in 1528 as a private chapel for Sir Thomas More, who in c. 1520 settled in the area. He and his family regularly worshipped at the church, which was just a short stroll away from their palatial home, of which no trace remains today. Surrounded by formal gardens and orchards, the house once stood on the site of the present-day Beaufort Street, and stretched from the river to the present King's Road.

More's private chapel was virtually the only section of the church to remain standing after the air raid. In the years that followed the 1941 attack, the church was lovingly and meticulously rebuilt, and appears much as it did before the war. Many of the memorials shattered in the blast were painstakingly restored, and the remains of ancient tombs, salvaged from the rubble, returned to their rightful place within the church, including that of Lady Jane Guildford, Duchess of Northumberland. Lady Jane was the mother of, among others, Robert Dudley, Earl of Leicester, and his younger brother, Guildford Dudley, who in 1553 married Lady Jane Grey.

Other Tudor monuments include that of Gregory Fiennes, Lord Dacre, and his wife, Anne, Lady Dacre, who died in 1594 and 1595 respectively, and a memorial to Sir Thomas More,

Chelsea Old Church, 2012. The original church, where Thomas More and family regularly worshipped, was largely destroyed in 1941, but lovingly rebuilt after the war. (Author's collection)

Statue of Thomas More made by L. Cubitt Bevis, Chelsea Old Church, 2012. (Author's collection)

which bears an inscription written by More, describing his life and ending with a tribute to his first and second wives, Jane Colt and Alice Harpur.

In the chancel is a memorial to the Hungerford family, below which is the tomb of Sir Edmund Bray (d. 1539). Other highlights include the sixteenth-century triumphal arch and the capitals of the pillars leading into the chancel, which Hans Holbein is said to have designed.

As you exit the church, look out for the statue of Sir Thomas More made by L. Cubitt Bevis in 1969, and just across the road from the west door of the church is Roper's Garden, which is believed to have once formed part of the gardens of More's vast Chelsea estate.

Visitor Information

The church is open from 2–4 p.m. on Tuesdays, Wednesdays and Thursdays, however, I recommend contacting the Parish Office ahead of your visit to confirm these hours.

The nearest underground stations are South Kensington and Sloane Square. The latter is about a 15-minute walk from the church. Alight at Sloane Square, exit the station onto King's Road and follow it to Old Church Street. Turn left and follow the road all the way to the river, where you'll see the church on your left.

No doubt the very Tudor-looking house across Roper's Garden will catch your attention. This is Crosby Hall, a largely twentieth-century house constructed by Christopher Moran to house a spectacular medieval survivor – a fifteenth-century great hall. Between 1466 and 1475, Sir John Crosby built a grand home in Bishopsgate. During the sixteenth century, the house was occupied by a number of prominent statesmen, including Sir Thomas More. The hall was moved to its present site in 1910, and Mr Moran's private house built to house it.

While in the area, you might also like to visit the site of Chelsea Place, a former royal manor where it's likely that Henry VIII and Jane Seymour celebrated their betrothal on 20 May 1536, just one day after Anne Boleyn's execution. Catherine Howard visited the house during her brief reign, and Katherine Parr was given the property in 1544 as part of her dower. It became Katherine's principal residence after Henry VIII's death, and the backdrop to her illicit love affair with Thomas Seymour. The Tudor house also witnessed the death of Anne of Cleves, on 16 July 1557. Sadly, the manor was demolished in the 1750s – a blue plaque next to 25 Cheyne Walk marks its approximate location.

The fine Tudor houses that once lined this fashionable area of London all boasted sumptuous gardens, which served more than simply a decorative function. Plants and herbs were grown as food but many, including lavender and rosemary, were also used for medicinal purposes. Interestingly, just a short walk from the church stands one of London's oldest botanic gardens, founded in 1673 as the Apothecaries' Garden. Chelsea Physic Garden boasts an extensive plant collection, including a Garden of Medicinal Plants. For opening times and other visitor information, go to www.chelseaphysicgarden.co.uk

To check church opening hours visit www.chelseaoldchurch.org.uk/

Chelsea Old Church postcode: SW3 5LT

Christchurch Greyfriars Church Garden stands on the site of the thirteenth-century Franciscan Church of Greyfriars, a favoured burial place for the upper echelons of medieval London society, including royalty, duchesses, dukes, earls and knights.

The original church was rebuilt on a grand scale in the early fourteenth century, at the behest of one of its main benefactors, Margaret of France, second queen consort of Edward I, who was buried there in 1318. Before the close of the century, two more queens would be interred there, Joan of England (also known as Joan of the Tower), Queen of Scotland and daughter of Edward II, and her mother, Queen Isabella, the infamous 'She-Wolf of France'. The heart of Eleanor of Provence, queen consort of Henry III, was also buried there.

In addition to the magnificent church – the largest in London after St Paul's Cathedral – the monastery boasted a fine library, which became a flourishing centre of learning during the fourteenth and fifteenth centuries.

In 1534, Elizabeth Barton, known as 'the Holy Maid of Kent', was buried in the churchyard after being executed for treason at Tyburn, alongside a number of her supporters. She had predicted that if Henry VIII went ahead with his marriage to Anne Boleyn he would lose his kingdom and 'die a villain's death', prophecies which eventually led to her execution.

Greyfriars was dissolved in 1538, after which the Greyfriars Church became a parish church. In 1552, during the reign of Edward VI, Christ's Hospital was founded in the former monastic buildings, for the care and education of poor and orphaned children. Tragically, both the school and the medieval

Christchurch Greyfriars Church Garden, 2016. (Author's collection)

church were lost during the Great Fire of 1666. A new church, designed by Christopher Wren, was built on the site in the late seventeenth/early eighteenth centuries, only to be largely destroyed by incendiary bombs during the Second World War. The west tower and some sections of wall are all that survive.

Today, a delightful cottage garden occupies the site of the former nave of the church, the ten wooden towers representing the pillars that once held up the building's roof. On weekdays, when the weather is fine, Londoners can usually be found enjoying their lunch breaks in this tranquil and picturesque place. One wonders if they're aware of the site's long history or that beneath their feet lie the remains of hundreds of people, including three medieval queens and a doomed religious visionary.

Visitor Information

Christchurch Greyfriars Church Garden is permanently open and located on the corner of King Edward Street and Newgate Street, just a few minutes walk from St Paul's Cathedral. The nearest underground station is St Paul's.

The buildings adjacent to the garden, on King Edward Street (known as Stinking or Chick Lane in Tudor times), roughly occupy part of the site of the monastery's extensive gardens and Great Cloister, where the library once stood.

For information on hiring the garden, visit www.cityoflondon.gov.uk/things-to-do/green-spaces/city-gardens/visitor-information/Pages/christchurch-greyfriars-church-garden.aspx

Postcode: EC1A 7BA

Lying on the south bank of the River Thames, close to London Bridge, is the Cathedral and Collegiate Church of St Saviour and St Mary Overie (or Overy), better known as Southwark Cathedral. It has been a site of Christian worship for more than a millennium, but was only elevated to cathedral status in 1905, when the diocese of Southwark was created.

The first written reference to a 'Monasterium' on the site is found in the Domesday Book, the great land survey of England (and a small part of what is now Wales) commissioned by William the Conqueror in December 1085. It's possible, though, that the origins of the site date back even further, as legend has it that a House of Sisters, dedicated to the Virgin Mary, was founded on the site in 606, and replaced by Swithun, Bishop of Winchester, with a college of priests in the ninth century. This tradition was recorded in the survey of London made by the Elizabethan historian John Stowe, who claimed that there had been a community of nuns on the site 'long before the [Norman] conquest'.

In 1106, in the reign of King Henry I, two Norman knights, William Dauncy and William Pont de l'Arche, refounded the church as an Augustinian Priory. As the church was dedicated to St Mary, and situated on the south side of the Thames, it later became known as St Mary Overy ('over the river'). The Augustinians highly valued public service, and so a hospital was built to the south of the church to serve the needs of the community's sick and poor, which was later dedicated to St Thomas Becket of Canterbury.

A devastating fire that started on London Bridge in July 1212 destroyed much of the area, including the priory and hospital. Hundreds of Londoners, or possibly even thousands as recorded by Stowe, are reported to have perished in the blaze, with the greatest loss of life occurring on the bridge itself, where many people became trapped.

The hospital was rebuilt on what is now Borough High Street, and remained there until 1862, at which time it was temporarily moved to Walworth, before occupying its present site in Lambeth. The priory was rebuilt in the new Gothic style of architecture, which had emerged from northern France in the middle of the twelfth century and was characterised by the use of the pointed arch, ribbed vaults and flying buttresses.

In 1539, the priory was surrendered to Henry VIII, and the following year the church was reopened as the Parish Church of St Saviour. During the reign of Mary I, it was home to a bishop's court, where the Bishop of Winchester, Stephen Gardiner, and the Bishop of London, Edmund Bonner, conducted heresy trials. Among those tried and convicted to be burned there were Bishop John Hooper, John Rogers, John Bradford, Robert Ferrer, Rowland Taylor and Laurence Saunders.

Throughout the reign of Elizabeth I, the church continued to serve its colourful parishioners who included foreign craftsmen and traders, merchants, actors – including William Shakespeare – and prostitutes from the Bankside brothels. As it was situated outside the jurisdiction of the City, Tudor Southwark, a predominantly poor and crowded area, quickly became the city's entertainment district, and the red-light district too, home to countless taverns, gambling, bear-baiting, theatres and brothels. In his survey of London, Stowe described some of its features:

> On the banke of the Riuer Thames there is now a continuall building of tenements, about halfe a mile in length to the bridge. Then from the Bridge straight towardes the South a continuall streete, called long Southwarke, builded on both sides with diuers lanes

Southwark Cathedral, 2016.
(Author's collection)

and alleyes ... there be two Beare gardens, the olde and new places, wherein be kept Beares, Buls and other beastes to be bayted. As also Mastiues in seuerall kenels, nourished to baite them. These Beares and other Beasts are there bayted in plottes of ground, scaffolded about for the Beholders to stand safe ... Next on this banke was sometime the Bordello or stewes, a place so called, of certaine stew houses priuiledged there, for the repaire of incontinent men to the like women ...

Adding to the borough's notoriety were five prisons: the Clink, the Marshalsea, the King's Bench, the White Lion and the Borough Compter. As for the playhouses, by the end of the Tudor reign there were three main theatres in Southwark: the Rose, the Globe and the Swan.

The actor and playwright William Shakespeare lived for a time in Southwark, close to the Globe Theatre, and as previously mentioned, worshipped at the Parish Church of St Saviour. On the morning of 31 December 1607, Shakespeare's younger brother, Edmund, was laid to rest there, with William almost certainly in attendance. While the exact location of his grave is unknown, he is commemorated by a memorial stone in the floor of the choir.

Over the years, various repairs and alterations have been made to the church, including the rebuilding of the nave in the late nineteenth century. The area was heavily damaged during the Second World War, with more than 1,600 bombs dropped on Southwark between October 1940 and June 1941, however, thankfully, the ancient cathedral emerged relatively unscathed.

Today, Southwark Cathedral is home to many treasures, including monuments, tombs and artworks. One can easily spend a couple of hours exploring the church's beautiful interior, which is sure to delight all history lovers. On the west walls, look out for examples of the original fifteenth-century roof bosses, originally in the nave ceiling, and near the baptismal font you'll find remnants of the medieval arcading.

In the north aisle is the elaborate tomb of the poet John Gower (d. 1408). His full-sized recumbent effigy rests its head on his three most famous works, written in Latin, French and English, *Confessio Amantis*, *Speculum Meditantis* (or *Mirour de l'omme*) and *Vox Clamantis*.

Opposite, in the south aisle, is Christopher Webb's Shakespeare's window, which depicts characters from Shakespeare's plays, and below the window, a lovely monument to the Bard carved by Henry McCarthy in 1912 and set against the background of seventeenth-century Southwark. Shakespeare's recumbent alabaster figure is shown at rest in a Bankside meadow and in his hand he holds a sprig of rosemary as a sign of remembrance.

Keep an eye out for the memorial to Wenceslas Hollar, the seventeenth-century engraver from Prague, whose famous *Long View of London* was drawn from the top of the cathedral's tower in 1647.

Opposite the fine memorial to Richard Humble and his two wives is the carved wooden effigy of a thirteenth-century knight, and nearby, the stunning sixteenth-century Nonsuch Chest, a gift from the Offley family in 1588, previously used to store parish records.

The tomb of Bishop Lancelot Andrewes is another of the cathedral's highlights. He was an English bishop and a noted scholar, who served both Elizabeth I and her successor, James I. In the latter's reign, Andrewes oversaw the translation of the Old Testament for the King James Bible, released in 1611.

A highlight is the magnificent high-altar screen, originally erected by Bishop Richard Fox in 1520, and restored in the nineteenth and twentieth centuries. The statues were added from 1905 onwards, and depict people with a connection to Southwark, including Saint Swithun, Saint Thomas Becket and the poet John Gower.

The Retro Choir, redesigned by Sir Ninian Comper in 1930, is the oldest part of the cathedral. It was here that the heresy trials were conducted in the reign of Mary I.

Finally, if time and weather permit, be sure to spend some time exploring the churchyard and herb garden, where you'll discover a selection of herbs and plants that would have been

grown in the gardens of the medieval priory and used by the Augustinian canons to treat the sick.

Visitor Information

Southwark Cathedral is situated just a few minutes walk from London Bridge underground station, in an area rich in history. It's easy to spend a day or two exploring Bankside's many historical attractions.

If you're visiting the cathedral on a weekday or on a Saturday, then I recommend you take a stroll through Borough Market, London's renowned food and drink market, which has existed in one form or another for around 1,000 years! With well over 100 stalls to choose from, it's the perfect destination for food lovers.

Just around the corner from the cathedral is the *Golden Hinde*, a full-sized replica of the Tudor ship Sir Francis Drake used to circumnavigate the globe between 1577 and 1580, and just a few paces away from the reconstructed Tudor galleon you'll find the remains of Winchester Palace.

Constructed in the thirteenth century, it was one of the most important buildings of medieval London and home to the powerful Bishops of Winchester. Unfortunately, the palace was largely destroyed by fire in 1814, and all that survives today are segments

Ruins of Winchester Palace, Southwark, 2016. (Author's collection)

of wall from the Great Hall, which can be viewed from the pavement on Clink Street.

If you're interested in finding out more about the Clink, one of England's most notorious prisons, then you might like to visit the Clink Prison Museum, situated just a short walk away from the ruins of Winchester Palace.

Finally, very close to the above museum, are the Rose Playhouse and the Globe Theatre. The Rose hosts open days most Saturdays, where you can find out more about the Elizabethan playhouse that once stood on the site, and learn about the excavations carried out in the area. They also frequently stage Shakespeare's plays, full details are available on their website.

The Globe Theatre is a reconstruction of its Tudor predecessor and, since its opening in 1997, has been home to public talks, lectures, performances and a wonderful exhibition exploring the history of the iconic Globe Theatre, and the life of its most famous playwright – William Shakespeare.

For cathedral opening times and other visitor information, please visit www.cathedral.southwark.anglican.org

For information about the historic Borough Market, visit www.boroughmarket.org.uk

To find out more about visiting the *Golden Hinde*, go to www.goldenhinde.com

For opening times and information about tours of the Clink Prison Museum, visit www.clink.co.uk.

For information on open days and upcoming events at the Rose Playhouse go to www.roseplayhouse.org.uk

To learn more about the Globe Exhibition and Tour, and to find out about upcoming performances, visit www.shakespearesglobe.com

Southwark Cathedral postcode: SE1 9DA

In 1123 Rahere, a courtier turned monk who served William the Conqueror's fourth son, Henry I, founded the Church of St Bartholomew the Great, as part of a monastery of Augustinian canons. Alongside the priory church, Rahere also constructed residential buildings for the canons, and a hospital, known today as Barts, which has been caring for the sick on its present site in Smithfield for almost 900 years.

Smithfield, originally 'smoothfield', was located outside the city walls, and over the centuries has provided the backdrop to historic revolts, famous fairs and jousting tournaments, including a spectacular tournament held in 1467, which saw Anthony Woodville, brother of Queen Elizabeth Woodville, defeat Anthony, the Bastard of Burgundy.

During the religious turmoil of the sixteenth century, Smithfield was one of London's main execution sites, where hundreds perished for their faith, including Anne Askew, a Protestant martyr and poet, who was found guilty of heresy and burnt at the stake on 16 July 1546. She is the only woman on record to have been tortured at the Tower of London, allegedly racked by Sir Richard Rich and Sir Thomas Wriothesley.

In 1539, Prior Robert Fuller surrendered the monastery to Henry VIII, who ordered that the nave of the church be demolished. He granted the monastic buildings to the unscrupulous Sir Richard Rich, and retained the canons' choir and sanctuary for parish use. Under Mary I, a Dominican convent was established at St Bartholomew's, however, this was dissolved by Elizabeth I in July 1559, at which time the church became again a parish church, as it had been in the reign of Elizabeth's half brother, Edward VI.

As for the hospital, this was allowed to continue after the dissolution of the priory, although, its source of income had disappeared and so its future hung in the balance. The citizens of London, concerned about what would become of the sick and destitute, petitioned the king to grant the City four

hospitals, and so finally, in December 1546, St Bartholomew's Hospital was granted to the City of London, along with Bethlem, Bridewell and St Thomas'. In January 1547, just before his death, Henry also endowed the hospital with properties and income.

The hospital escaped damage during the Great Fire of 1666 but was rebuilt in the eighteenth century. Like the hospital, the priory church survived the Great Fire, and for the next two centuries, parts of the building were turned over to secular use. The fourteenth-century Lady Chapel, for example, being used as a house, a printing press and a lace and fringe factory. In the nineteenth century, a process of restoration began that continues to this day.

The main entry to the church today is via a magnificent Elizabethan gatehouse, which was built above the original west door of the nave, demolished in 1539. To your right, as you walk towards the entry, once stood the main cloister, and beyond, the Chapter House, Prior's Lodgings and other monastic buildings.

Once inside the church there are a number of interesting features to look out for, including the shrine-tomb of the founder Prior Rahere, which dates to the early fifteenth century, and Prior Bolton's beautiful oriel window that overlooks the high altar. William Bolton was prior of St Bartholomew's from 1505 until his death in 1532. He was an educated man and a respected builder, who worked on Westminster Abbey and also carried out building work at St Bartholomew's. Bolton's lodgings adjoined the triforium, and so the window allowed him to see Mass being celebrated at the high altar, and keep an eye on the canons in their stalls below.

St Bartholomew the Great, West Smithfield, 2016. The church was founded in the twelfth century, as part of a monastery of Augustinian canons, which was surrendered to Henry VIII in 1539. (Author's collection)

The Tudor Gatehouse, St Bartholomew
the Great, West Smithfield, 2016.

In the south aisle is the grand Elizabethan tomb of Sir Walter Mildmay, who founded Emmanuel College in Cambridge and served as chancellor and sub-treasurer of the Exchequer under Elizabeth I, and his wife, Lady Mary Mildmay. Nearby, is a late Tudor monument to Percival and Agnes Smallpace, and opposite, a fine monument to Sir Robert Chamberlayne, who died in 1615. Look out also for the font, which dates from 1405 and is said to be one of only two pre-Reformation fonts in London, the other is housed at St Dunstan's in Stepney.

Much of the priory's cloister was lost after the Dissolution, however, a small section survives and is today home to the Cloister Café, a wonderfully atmospheric setting for a meal.

Stepping into the hushed and breathtaking interiors of St Bartholomew's is truly an exercise in time travel, so it's little wonder that over the years the church has been featured in many period films, including *Shakespeare in Love* in 1998, *Elizabeth: The Golden Age* in 2007 and *The Other Boleyn Girl* in 2008.

Visitor Information

Just a short walk from St Bartholomew the Great is another place worth noting, St Bartholomew's Hospital Museum, which is set in the historic north wing of the hospital, and entered via the Henry VIII Gate on Giltspur Street. Be sure to look up above the gateway, where you'll find an early eighteenth-century statue of King Henry VIII, said to be the only outdoor statue of the king in London.

Situated on the hospital grounds and very close to the museum is St Bartholomew the Less, which was established to serve the hospital. It has been significantly altered and refurbished over the centuries but retains its fifteenth-century tower and a section of medieval wall.

Finally, adjacent to the churchyard, at 41–42 Cloth Fair stands another remarkable survivor, a building thought to have been built between 1597 and 1614, and one of only a handful of houses to escape the ravages of the fire. It was heavily restored in the twentieth century and is today privately owned.

For information on visiting St Bartholomew the Less, go to www.greatstbarts.com/Pages/Family_Mass/Fammass.html

For museum opening times, visit www.bartshealth.nhs.uk/about-us/museums,-history-and-archives/st-bartholomews-museum

For St Bartholomew the Great and The Cloister Café opening times and other visitor information, please visit www.greatstbarts.com

Postcode: EC1A 9DS

Early eighteenth-century statue of King Henry VIII, St Bartholomew Hospital, 2016. (Author's collection)

St Dunstan-in-the-West is an Anglican church situated on Fleet Street in London. While its origins date back to medieval times, being first founded between 988 and 1070, the present-day church was built in 1831–32. The church's tower, however, was rebuilt in 1950, after it was damaged by German bombers in 1944.

If you're wondering why a predominantly late Georgian/ early Victorian building has been included in a book about Tudor London, it's because in a niche above the vestry door in the small courtyard adjacent to the church stands a truly remarkable object, and one easily missed by passers by, the only known surviving statue of Queen Elizabeth I carved during her lifetime. This Tudor treasure is also said to be the oldest outdoor statue in London.

The statue, which probably dates from 1586, originally stood on Ludgate, the westernmost gate of the city wall, just a short walk east from the church, towards St Paul's Cathedral. Having been badly damaged in the Great Fire of 1666, the gate was demolished in 1760, and the statue of the last Tudor monarch was given to St Dunstan's.

When the church was rebuilt in the nineteenth century, the statue was stored in a nearby building and, unbelievably, forgotten for the better part of a decade. It was rediscovered in 1839, as reported by *The Times* and quoted in a short history of the church compiled by Robbie Millen:

Statue of Queen Elizabeth I,
St Dunstan-in-the-West, 2016.
(Author's collection)

This Statue of
QUEEN ELIZABETH
formerly stood on the West side of LUDGATE.
That Gate being taken down in 1760 to open the Street
was given by the CITY to S.ʳ FRANCIS GOSLING, KN.ᵗ
ALDERMAN of this WARD, who caused it to be placed here.

The workmen engaged some time in taking down an old public-house adjoining St Dunstan's Church Fleet Street discovered in one of the cellars the ancient stone statue of Queen Elizabeth which formerly stood in the nave of the old church. The Parochial authorities have resolved to place it on the south end of the church facing Fleet Street.

The statue was later repaired and restored to its former glory, and unveiled by Dame Millicent Fawcett, a leading Suffragist and campaigner for equal rights for women, in a ceremony at St Dunstan's. Fawcett also left a £700 legacy in her will for its continued upkeep.

The statue of the mythical King Lud (after which Ludgate is thought to have been named), which stands beneath that of Elizabeth's, once decorated the eastern face of Ludgate. It too found its way to St Dunstan's after the gate was demolished.

As for the interior of the church, keep an eye out for some ancient monuments which predate the rebuilding of the church, including the two brass kneeling figures of Henry Dacres, 'Citizen and Merchant Tailor and sometime Alderman of London ...' [spelling modernised], and his wife, Elizabeth.

Ludgate from the west, as it probably appeared in the sixteenth century, by H.W. Brewer. The spire of St Mary Overie (or Overy), the present-day Southwark Cathedral, can be seen across the river. (Author's collection)

Visitor Information

The nearest underground stations are Chancery Lane and Temple. While in the area, take a stroll up Fleet Street towards St Paul's Cathedral, stopping at 143 Fleet Street, where you'll find, at first-floor level, an early twentieth-century statue of Mary, Queen of Scots. At the time of writing, it stood directly above Pret A Manger and next door to Ye Olde Cheshire Cheese, a historic pub rebuilt shortly after the Great Fire.

Speaking of ancient pubs, across the road and slightly west of St Dunstan's (and just around the corner from the beautiful twelfth-century Temple Church) is Ye Old Cock Tavern. This ancient watering hole has its origins in Tudor times, and over the years has welcomed some famous names, including Samuel Pepys, Oliver Goldsmith, Charles Dickens and Alfred, Lord Tennyson. To book a table, visit www.taylor-walker.co.uk/pub/ye-olde-cock-tavern-holborn/c1188

Visit the official site of St Dunstan's in the West for opening times and information on services and events: www.stdunstaninthewest.org

Postcode: EC4A 2HR

St Etheldreda's Church is located on Ely Place, just a stone's throw from Holborn Circus, on land once occupied by Ely Palace, also known as Ely Place or House, the London residence of the Bishops of Ely. In its heyday, the sprawling episcopal complex of some 58 acres boasted splendid apartments, a fine hall, a chapel, orchards, vineyards and gardens renowned for their fields of saffron and strawberries. However, all that survives today, albeit in an altered state, is the former private chapel of the Bishops of Ely completed in around 1290 and dedicated to St Etheldreda, the Saxon princess who founded Ely Cathedral in Cambridgeshire.

It's possible that Henry VIII and Katherine of Aragon worshipped at the chapel in November 1531, when they attended a feast for the newly made serjeants-at-law, which extended over five days at Ely Palace, from Friday, 10 November to Tuesday, 14 November. In his *Survey of London*, John Stow recorded that 'in this house for the large and commodious rooms thereof, divers great and solemn feasts have been kept ...'. Including in the year 1531, when King Henry VIII and Queen Katherine dined there but in separate chambers. The king had been for some time enamoured with Anne Boleyn and actively pursuing to annul his marriage to Katherine. It's likely that the estranged royal couple did not even cross paths while guests of Bishop Nicholas West.

Stow also shared details of the great amount of food that was consumed over the celebrations, including '24 great beefs', '1 carcass of an ox', '100 fat muttons', '51 great veals', '91 pigs', and dozens of capons, pigeons, pullets, swans and larks, remarking that it resembled the abundance of food served at a coronation feast.

After the Reformation the chapel was used for Anglican worship before briefly being returned to the old faith under Mary I. In *c.* 1576, Elizabeth I demanded that Bishop Richard Cox lease a portion of the house and lands to one of her

St Etheldreda's Church, 2016. The thirteenth-century church is all that survives today of Ely Palace, the London residence of the Bishops of Ely. (Author's collection)

favourites, Sir Christopher Hatton, which he did after much protestation. Hatton went on to spend a considerable amount of money on enhancing the property and died there in 1591. His connection to the area is recalled by nearby Hatton Garden, London's historic jewellery quarter.

The palace survived the Great Fire of London, however, it was by then falling into disrepair. It was partly demolished after the Civil War when it was requisitioned by Parliament for use as a prison and hospital, and in 1772 it was sold to the Crown who subsequently sold it to one Charles Cole. He later built the present-day Ely Place with its row of Georgian houses, on the site of the few remaining palace buildings, and made alterations to the chapel, which he preserved as a place of Anglican worship for Ely Place's affluent residents.

In 1820, the chapel passed to the National Society for the Education of the Poor, and changed hands several more times before the Roman Catholic priest Father William Lockhart purchased it at auction in 1873, the ban on Catholic worship having been lifted by the Catholic Emancipation Act of 1829. Soon after, Father Lockhart embarked on an extensive restoration project that would strip away centuries of unsympathetic alterations and restore the chapel to its medieval glory.

When you step inside St Etheldreda's today, you're immediately struck by the sheer beauty of the chapel, and by the ancient silence that embraces you. There is no denying that this is a special place, a tranquil haven that has withstood

the test of time and survived centuries of use, civil conflict, a raging inferno and two world wars. It is a beautiful and contemplative space that feels miles away from the hubbub of the world.

The stunning stained glass windows are modern replacements for those lost over the years. On the corbels between the windows stand eight statues of sixteenth-century martyrs, made by May Blakeman between 1962 and 1964, along with statues of the Virgin Mary and St Etheldreda to the left and right of the high altar, respectively.

The statues of martyrs on the south wall (on your right when facing the high altar), represent John Forest (d. 1538), Margaret

An illustration by H.W. Brewer of Ely
Place, as it is likely to have appeared
in the sixteenth century. The bishop's
chapel in the foreground is the
present-day St Etheldreda's Church.
The tall spire on the top left is that of
St John's Priory, Clerkenwell, behind
which stands the Charterhouse.
(Author's collection)

Ward (d. 1588), Swithin Wells (d. 1591) and Edmund Jennings
(d. 1591) nearest the statue of St Etheldreda. On the opposite
wall are Edmund Jones (d. 1590), John Roche (d. 1588), Anne
Line (d. 1601) and John Houghton (d. 1535).

While the palace buildings and extensive gardens and
meadows are gone, the chapel is an architectural and historic
jewel, and one most certainly worth visiting.

Visitor Information

St Etheldreda's is situated on Ely Place, a gated cul-
de-sac off Charterhouse Street near Holborn Circus.
The nearest underground stations are Chancery Lane
and Farringdon.

This well-hidden historic gem, which lays claim to
being the oldest Roman Catholic Church in England,
and one of only two surviving buildings in London
from the reign of Edward I, is tucked in between two
townhouses and barely visible until you are standing
right in front of it.

While in the area I also recommend dropping
into Ye Olde Mitre, an eighteenth-century pub with
possibly Tudor origins, tucked away down a lane off

Ely Place. If you miss the entryway on Ely Place, which is on the same side as the church and back towards Charterhouse Street, it can also be accessed via a laneway between 8 and 9 Hatton Garden. Find out more at www.yeoldemitreholborn.co.uk

Visit the official site of St Etheldreda's for opening times and other visitor information: www.stetheldreda.com

Postcode: EC1N 6RY

In the heart of the City of London, just off Bishopsgate, you'll find St Helen's. Its unorthodox design is on account of the fact that in the early thirteenth century, a convent for nuns of the Benedictine order was established on the grounds, and a new church built for their use to the north of the existing twelfth-century parish church, and so, unusually, the church has two parallel naves. A fifteenth-century arcade that dominates the church today, and which was originally screened to give the nuns privacy while at worship, separates the Nun's Choir and the parish church.

In November 1538, the priory was surrendered to King Henry VIII, after which the 'Nonnes Churche of Seynt Helyns' and its extensive monastic buildings were granted to Richard Williams, also known as Richard Cromwell. He was the son of Morgan Williams and Katherine Cromwell, who was the elder sister of Henry VIII's powerful chief minister, Thomas Cromwell. In 1543, Williams sold the priory buildings and church to the Leathersellers' Company, and over the next two centuries, minor repairs and alterations were made to the church. The monastic buildings, however, did not fare as well, and by 1799, they had all been destroyed.

St Helen's was one of only a handful of London churches to survive both the Great Fire of 1666 and the Blitz during the Second World War, however, it was damaged by IRA bombs that detonated nearby in 1992 and 1993. Although the damage was significant, it was eventually repaired and the interior of the church redesigned by the architect Quinlan Terry.

Among the many attractions of St Helen's are its collection of brasses and fifteenth and sixteenth-century monuments, said to be second in number only to Westminster Abbey, earning the church the appellation 'Westminster Abbey of the City'. These include splendid monuments to Sir John Crosby (d. 1476), merchant, diplomat and politician, and his wife Agnes; Sir William Pickering (d. 1574) who, among other posts,

St Helen's, Bishopsgate, Great
St Helen's, London, 2016.
(Author's collection)

served as the English ambassador to France in the reign of Edward VI; Sir Thomas Gresham (d. 1579), founder of the Royal Exchange, and Sir Julius Caesar (d. 1636), who held various posts during the reign of Elizabeth I, including senior judge of the High Court of Admiralty.

Look out also for a grand monument to Sir John Spencer (d. 1610), merchant and one-time Lord Mayor of London, and several Elizabethan monuments with kneelers. A colourful nineteenth-century window commemorates William Shakespeare, who was a parishioner for a time in the 1590s.

Visitor Information

St Helen's is located on Great St Helen's Street, in the shadow of 30 St Mary Axe, also known as the Gherkin. It is usually open to visitors from Monday to Friday between 9.30 a.m. and 12.30 p.m., however, as I found it closed on several occasions during normal opening hours, I recommend phoning or emailing ahead of your visit to avoid disappointment.

While in the area, you might also like to visit another miraculous survivor of the Great Fire of London and the Blitz, St Andrew Undershaft Church, located on the corner of Leadenhall and St Mary Axe. The largely Tudor building is home to a memorial to John Stow, who wrote *The Survey of London* in 1598. Today, the church is primarily used by St Helen's Church for meetings and functions, and is normally closed to the public, however, you can arrange a visit by contacting St Helen's Church Office.

The nearest underground stations are Liverpool Street, Bank, Monument and Aldgate.

To check opening hours and/or request a visit to St Andrew Undershaft Church, visit www.st-helens.org.uk or email: st-helens@st-helens.org.uk

Postcode: EC3A 6AT

The Parish Church of St Magnus the Martyr is situated on Lower Thames Street, close to London Bridge. This is, though, not the first bridge to have traversed the Thames here. By the early eleventh century, a wooden bridge had been built across the river, a factor which triggered an influx of craftsmen and traders to the area, necessitating the building of a church to serve the community's spiritual needs.

St Magnus was founded some time in the late eleventh or early twelfth century in response to the area's swelling population, and by 1209, a new stone bridge had been built to replace its wooden predecessor. For more than 600 years, St Magnus's churchyard formed part of the approach to Old London Bridge, which until 1831 was aligned with Fish Street Hill.

In Tudor times, anyone travelling south across the stone bridge, or entering the City from the south, passed right by the west door of the church. The regular traffic jams on the overcrowded bridge meant that Londoners and travellers often had to wait in this space before being allowed to cross, and so it hummed with activity for most of the day. As crowds were almost always guaranteed in this bustling corner of town, known as St Magnus Corner, it was also where notices were posted and public proclamations read.

The church narrowly escaped destruction in 1633, when a fire broke out in a house at the north end of London Bridge, only to be destroyed in the Great Fire of London, which began in Thomas Faryner's bakery on Pudding Lane – just a few hundred metres away from the church – just after midnight on 2 September 1666.

St Magnus was rebuilt between 1671 and 1687, under the direction of Sir Christopher Wren, who after the catastrophic blaze was in charge of rebuilding more than fifty London churches in addition to St Paul's Cathedral. In the middle of

the eighteenth century, the buildings that lined London Bridge were dismantled to widen the roadway and a new pedestrian walkway was built along the east side of the bridge. As a result, the west end of the church was altered.

In 1831, the ancient bridge, which in the sixteenth and seventeenth centuries was considered one of the world's great wonders, was demolished and a new bridge opened up west of the original site. Its destruction heralded the end of St Magnus the Martyr's role as gateway to the City of London.

As an interesting side note, the 'new bridge' was sold to an American by the name of Robert McCulloch in 1968, and reconstructed in Lake Havasu City, Arizona, where it can be seen today. As for the present-day London Bridge, it was opened by Queen Elizabeth II in 1973.

Of particular interest inside the church is an extraordinary 4m-long model of Old London Bridge, as it would have appeared in around 1400, made by David T. Aggett in 1987.

In the small quiet churchyard, it's difficult to imagine that this was once a hive of activity. Just think of all the people who've passed by this very spot on their way in and out of the City. All the Tudor monarchs and their courtiers would have been familiar with the church and ridden by it when travelling by road to the royal palace in Greenwich. Look out for stones from Old London Bridge and an ancient piece of wood, said to have once formed part of a Roman wharf.

St Magnus the Martyr, 2016.
(Author's collection)

Visitor Information

St Magnus the Martyr is usually open to visitors from 10–4 p.m. on Tuesday to Friday. The nearest underground station is Monument.

Just a short walk away from the church, on Fish Street Hill is the Monument to the Great Fire of London, built between 1671 and 1677 to commemorate

the Great Fire and celebrate the city's rebuilding. It stands on the site of St Margaret, the first church lost to the blaze, which unlike St Magnus was never rebuilt.

Across from this London icon is Pudding Lane, where a blue plaque on the corner of Pudding and Monument Street marks the approximate site of Thomas Faryner's bakery.

Visitors are welcome to climb the few hundred steps to the top of the Monument, to take in the panoramic views of London. For more information visit www.themonument.info

Visit the official site of St Magnus the Martyr for information on services and events: www.stmagnusmartyr.org.uk

Postcode: EC3R 6DN

A reconstruction of Old London Bridge from the south, as it appeared in Tudor times. In the foreground is St Mary Overie (or Overy), the present-day Southwark Cathedral. (Author's collection)

Standing between Westminster Abbey and the Houses of Parliament, St Margaret's Church was built in the latter part of the eleventh century as a parish church for the people of Westminster. The Benedictine monks of neighbouring Westminster Abbey found that the stream of local people wanting to hear Mass was interrupting their worship and so they built a smaller church next to the abbey to cater for the local community, and dedicated it to St Margaret of Antioch.

The nave of the church was replaced in the fourteenth century, but by the end of the fifteenth century the entire church was in a dilapidated state, and almost entirely rebuilt between 1482 and 1523. Despite further restorations in the eighteenth, nineteenth and twentieth centuries, the basic structure remains much the same as it was in Tudor times.

Inside the church there are a number of points of interest for the Tudor time traveller. Above the west doors are renaissance-style monuments commemorating two women who served Queen Elizabeth I: Blanche Parry, who is also buried in the church, and Lady Dorothy Stafford. The west window above the entrance dates from 1888 and commemorates the famous Elizabethan courtier and explorer, Sir Walter Raleigh, who was executed for treason in the Old Palace Yard of Westminster Palace in the reign of James I, and buried in the chancel of St Margaret's.

In the north aisle, keep an eye out for a painted stone bust commemorating Cornelius van Dun who died in 1577 aged 94. He served as a Yeoman of the Guard to four Tudor monarchs:

St Margaret's Church, Westminster, 2016. (Author's collection)

St Margaret's Church
Westminster Abbey

Visitors are welcome to this beautiful church
building, consecrated in 1523, is the third on the
St Margaret's has been the church of the Hou...

Windows commemorate Caxton an...
worshipped here, and Raleigh, who ...
of the altar, under the glorious ...
King Henry VIII and Catherine of ...

After about nine hundred years of w...
church for the people of Westminster
placed under the care of the ...
of Westminster by ...
It is still in reg...
and W...

Henry VIII, Edward VI, Mary I and Elizabeth I, and is depicted in his scarlet uniform.

While much of the stained glass at St Margaret's dates to the nineteenth and twentieth centuries, the magnificent east window contains some beautiful sixteenth-century Flemish glass (purchased by the church in 1758), commemorating Henry VIII's marriage to Katherine of Aragon. The king can be seen kneeling in the bottom left-hand corner, and Queen Katherine, in the opposite corner. We do not know what church the glass was originally intended for, however, Waltham Abbey or the Chapel of New Hall, renamed the Palace of Beaulieu by Henry VIII, have been suggested. Below the glorious window is the final resting place of Sir Walter Raleigh.

The south aisle is lined with many monuments, including a striking one to Mary, Lady Dudley, who died in 1600. Mary was a daughter of William Howard, 1st Baron Howard of Effingham, who was a great-uncle to Elizabeth I. Her second husband, Richard Montpesson, who erected the tomb, is depicted kneeling beside her.

On the south-west wall is Blanche Parry's marble and alabaster monument. Parry was the Chief Gentlewoman of Elizabeth I's privy chamber and also Keeper of the Queen's Jewels. She served Elizabeth faithfully for fifty-six years and was a friend and cousin of William Cecil, Lord Burghley.

Finally, to the west of the church, between Parliament Square and the path running parallel to Westminster Abbey, is the site of the original churchyard, where many hundreds of people were buried over the years, including William Caxton, the first English printer, in 1492. No sign of the graves remain today, as the area was grassed over in 1881.

As St Margaret's sits in the shadow of the mighty and awe-inspiring Westminster Abbey, visitors often overlook this historic church, however, it too has witnessed many important events in the history of England, and deserves its place on the Tudor trail.

Visitor Information

The nearest underground station is Westminster. For opening times and other visitor information, visit www.westminster-abbey.org/st-margarets-church
   Postcode: SW1P 3JX

St Olave's Church narrowly escaped being destroyed by the Great Fire of London. Samuel Pepys, who was a parishioner of the church, and who lived close by in the Navy Office buildings on Seething Lane, was an eyewitness to the catastrophic fire that devastated London in September 1666. On 6 September, he recorded in his *Diary* that at 'about two in the morning my wife calls me up and tells me of new cries of fire, it being come to Barking Church [All Hallows by the Tower], which is the bottom of our lane'.

The flames came within around 100m of St Olave's, and only a change in the direction of the wind – and perhaps the ingenious firebreak devised by Pepys and Sir William Penn – saved the ancient church from destruction.

As for the church's origins, it's thought to have been first built in the eleventh century, however, the first recorded reference to St Olave's – which is dedicated to St Olaf, patron saint of Norway – comes in the thirteenth century, in the will of Henry Le Botiner. At around this time, the presumably timber structure was rebuilt in stone and survived until around 1450 when it was again rebuilt by Richard and Robert Cely, as recorded by John Stow in his *Survey of London*. Stow also noted the 'fayre and large houses' that lined Seething Lane in the sixteenth century:

> In this Sidon lane [Seething Lane] diuers fayre and large houses are builded, namely one by Sir Iohn Allen, sometime Mayor of London, and of counsell vnto king Henry the eight: Sir Frances Walsingham Knight, Principal Secretary to the Queenes Maiestie that now is, was lodged there, and so was the Earle of Essex …

St Olave's was restored in 1632–33, as recorded in John Strype's *A Survey of the Cities of London and Westminster* published in 1720, and further extended later in the century.

As previously mentioned, it survived the Great Fire of London but was extensively damaged during the Blitz, at which time many of its ancient monuments were lost. Using as much of the original masonry as possible, the church was again rebuilt in the 1950s.

While much of the interior of St Olave's dates to the modern restoration, there survive some remnants of the medieval church, including a thirteenth-century crypt and sections of thirteenth- and fifteenth-century walls. There are also some interesting monuments to look out for, including those dedicated to the diarist Samuel Pepys and his wife, Elizabeth, who are buried in a vault beneath the nave, and those to Sir John and Lady Radcliffe, who died in 1568 and 1585 respectively.

The monument to Peter Turner (d. 1615), who was a physician at St Bartholomew's Hospital in the 1580s, went missing after the Second World War and was only recently recovered and reinstated. The most curious recorded burial at St Olave's, though, is that of one Mother Goose, who according to the burial registers was laid to rest on 14 September 1586.

Visitor Information

St Olave's is situated on the corner of Hart Street and Seething Lane, just a few minutes walk from Fenchurch Street Station. The nearest underground stations are Tower Hill and Monument.

The church is open most weekdays from 9 a.m. to 5 p.m., but is closed during the month of August and in the weeks following Christmas and Easter. I recommend that you contact the church office in advance to check whether the church will be open on the day you plan to visit.

You might also like to visit St Katharine Cree located on Leadenhall Street, about a 5-minute walk away.

The present building was largely constructed in the seventeenth century, however it was originally founded in the thirteenth century and retains a Tudor tower from its predecessor. The church is the final resting place of Sir Nicholas Throckmorton, an Elizabethan diplomat and politician, and is reputedly where the famous sixteenth-century portraitist Hans Holbein the Younger was buried in a communal pit, after dying of the plague in 1543.

To check opening hours for either church, visit www.sanctuaryinthecity.net

Postcode for St Olave's: EC3R 7NB

Postcode for St Katharine Cree: EC3A 3BP

In 1347, news reached England of a virulent and deadly disease that was spreading rapidly across Europe. It wasn't long before this disease, which most experts now believe was bubonic plague, arrived in England and decimated the country's population. The Black Death, as it became known from the 1800s onwards, gripped London in the autumn of 1348, and, over the next eighteen months or so, is estimated to have killed around half of the city's population. While it's impossible to ascertain the exact number of victims, the dead are believed to have numbered in the tens of thousands.

Existing cemeteries were quickly filled, and it became necessary to bury the corpses in mass graves in and around London. Sir Walter de Mauny, also known as Sir Walter de Manny, one of King Edward III's leading commanders, leased a plot of land in West Smithfield, from St Bartholomew's Priory, to use as a burial ground for plague victims, and built a chapel on the site. On this same land, he later established a Carthusian monastery, the Charterhouse. However, he died in January 1372, before the buildings were completed.

Over the next century, further buildings were added to the priory. In addition to the great cloister, around which stood the monks' two-storey lodgings or cells, and the priory church, a little cloister, boundary wall and gatehouse were constructed.

By the early sixteenth century, the London Charterhouse was a thriving community, attracting the likes of a young Thomas More, who spent time living there while studying law at nearby Lincoln's Inn. According to his son-in-law, William Roper, who wrote a biography of More in *c.* 1556, he 'gave himself to devotion and prayer in the Charterhouse of London, religiously living there without vow about four years ...'.

The Charterhouse's peace and prosperity came to an abrupt and violent end in May 1535, when its prior, John Houghton, was executed at Tyburn for denying the king's supremacy, alongside two other Carthusian priors, Robert Lawrence and Augustine Webster, and a Bridgettine monk from Syon Abbey, Richard Reynolds. According to the indictment, on 26 April 1535, while imprisoned at the Tower of London, all four men had declared, 'The King [Henry VIII] our sovereign lord is not supreme head on earth of the Church of England'. After suffering the full traitor's death, 'their quarters were hanged on the gates and walls of the city and on the gate of the Charterhouse'.

This did not, however, bring an end to the bloodshed. Over the next five years, another fifteen of London Charterhouse's monks met brutal ends, six were publicly executed, and nine others perished in Newgate Prison.

In November 1538, the monastery was suppressed, after which time it became crown property. Sir Edward North acquired the property in 1545, and constructed a grand house there, incorporating some of the monastic buildings, including the gatehouse and chapter house, which was adapted to serve as the chapel. Many of the other priory buildings, like the church, great cloister and little cloister, were demolished. In their place North built a new principal courtyard, today's Master's Court, and a secondary courtyard to the west, now Wash House Court.

Lord North's house was sumptuous enough to entertain royalty. On 23 November 1558, Elizabeth, the newly proclaimed 25-year-old Queen of England, stayed at the former priory for five days, while on her way from Hatfield House to London. Charles Wriothesley recorded the following details in his *Chronicle*:

Wednesday the 23 of November Queen Elizabeth came from Hatfield to the Lord North's house, in the late Charterhouse in London, the sheriffs of London meeting her Grace at the further end of Barnet town, within the shire of Middlesex, and so rode before her until she came to Charterhouse gate, where she remained till the Monday after [28 November].

This was not the queen's only visit to Lord North's house. In July 1561, Elizabeth spent four days at the Charterhouse, before departing on progress. The following is an extract from Strype's *Annals of the Reformation*:

> The 10th [of July], the queen came by water unto the Tower of London by twelve of the clock: her business now was to visit her mints, which she did in person; where she coined certain pieces of gold, and gave them away to several about her ... About five o'clock she went out at the iron gate, and so over Tower-hill unto Aldgate church; and so down Hounsditch to the Spital, and down Hoglane; and so over the fields unto the Charterhouse, being the lord North's place; attended in great state, (as was customary when she went abroad), before her, going on horseback, trumpeters, the gentlemen pensioners, the heralds of arms, the sergeants at arms; then gentlemen, then lords, and the lord Hunsdon bearing the sword immediately before the queen; after the queen the ladies riding. Here at the Charterhouse she tarried ...

On 13 July, the queen dined with William Cecil, her secretary of state, at his house near the Savoy, before riding back to the Charterhouse where she spent one more night, departing the following day 'on her progress into Essex'.

After Lord North's death in 1564, the Tudor mansion was sold to Thomas Howard, 4th Duke of Norfolk, a second cousin of the queen, and became known as Howard House. It served as the duke's principal London residence until he was executed for treason in June 1572.

The property exchanged hands a few more times, before the wealthy financier Thomas Sutton purchased it in 1611, and founded an almshouse on the site to cater for elderly men, known as 'Brothers', a function it still serves to this day. Alongside the almshouse, Sutton founded a school for boys, which flourished over the centuries and moved to its present site in Godalming, Surrey, in 1811.

Like so many of London's medieval buildings, the Charterhouse sustained extensive damage during the Second World War and was virtually completely destroyed. Only the chapel, the north side of Wash House Court and part of the great chamber escaped the inferno, which, thankfully, claimed no casualties.

While the architects John Seely and Paul Paget, best known for the restoration of the medieval Great Hall at Eltham Palace, are responsible for much of what we see today, there are some wonderful pre-war features to take note of.

The early fifteenth-century gateway, where Elizabeth was met with great pomp, survives, and today forms the main entrance to the Charterhouse. A section of the medieval boundary wall that once enclosed the priory also stands, and is visible to the right of the gateway.

In the entrance court, an archway leads to Sir Edward North's Master's Court, flanked by Wash House Court to the left (west) and Chapel Court to the right (east). The latter was the site of the priory church, demolished in 1545, and is today home to a memorial to the Carthusian martyrs.

The Tudor tourist will feel most at home in Wash House Court, a beautiful and tranquil courtyard where the history of the site is most palpable.

Other highlights include the Great Hall, which dates from the building of Sir Edward North's mansion in the mid-1540s and is home to a magnificent wooden screen installed by the 4th Duke of Norfolk in 1571, and the Norfolk Cloister, part of the original monastic cloister extended by Norfolk to create a covered approach to his tennis court.

The Great Chamber is another of the Charterhouse's many treasures. In Tudor times, this space was originally divided into two separate rooms. The elaborate fireplace was installed by the aforementioned duke, and embellished in the reign of Charles I. It was restored in 1955, after being extensively damaged during the war. Norfolk also added the bay on the north side of the chamber, and the decorated plaster ceiling, which was largely destroyed in 1941, with the exception of the ceiling in the bay itself, which is Tudor.

The chapel was originally the priory's chapter house, and dates from the early fifteenth century, with later additions, namely the north aisle, constructed in 1614. It houses the tomb of Charterhouse's founder, the philanthropic Thomas Sutton, who was greatly admired by many, including the English novelist

Daniel Defoe, who described the foundation of the almshouse and school as, 'the greatest and noblest gift that ever was given for charity, by any one man, public or private, in this nation'.

Visitor Information

Tours of the Charterhouse led by the brothers take place on Tuesdays, Wednesdays, Thursdays and every second Saturday at 2.15 p.m. These must be booked via the Charterhouse's website in advance of your visit.

In addition to the tours, from 2017, the Charterhouse will open its doors to the public for the first time in over 500 years. Visitors will be able to access a new

Wash House Court, the Charterhouse.
To the west of the new principal
courtyard, Sir Edward North
constructed a secondary courtyard,
known today as Wash House Court.
(Copyright Lawrence Watson, by kind
permission of the Charterhouse)

museum and the chapel, free of charge, from Tuesday to Sunday.

After touring this historic gem, be sure to spend some time wandering around Charterhouse Square. The private garden at its centre is the site of the Black Death burial pit, where thousands of medieval Londoners were buried.

Interestingly, during the sixteenth century, the square, or 'yard' as it was then known, was bounded on the east and south by fine houses, occupied by many prominent personalities of the day, including a string of French and Venetian ambassadors; John Leland, the English poet and antiquary, and a future queen of England. Katherine Parr, Henry's sixth and final consort, lived for a time with her second husband, John Latimer, roughly where Number 10 Charterhouse now stands.

The nearest underground stations are Barbican and Farringdon.

For opening times or to book a tour of the Charterhouse, please visit www.thecharterhouse.org

Postcode: EC1M 6AN

The Abbey [Westminster], one of the finest in the whole of England, is most magnificent and also very beautiful; it is renowned as the place of the coronation of the Kings of England and as their place of burial. It contains a large number of chapels and some very splendid royal monuments ...

From *The Diary of Baron Waldstein*

Steeped in more than 1,000 years of history, the Collegiate Church of St Peter, Westminster, more commonly known as Westminster Abbey, is a must-see for any history enthusiast. It has been a place of daily worship since about the middle of the tenth century, and the setting for every coronation since that of William the Conqueror's on Christmas Day 1066. Of the countless notable historical figures who have walked its ancient floors, many are also buried there, including all of the crowned Tudor monarchs, with the exception of Henry VIII who is buried in St George's Chapel, Windsor Castle, alongside his third wife, Jane Seymour.

A Little Background

In the middle of the eleventh century, Edward the Confessor, whose shrine remains at the heart of the abbey today, built a large stone church on the site of a small Benedictine monastery. This stood for 200 years, until 1245, when King Henry III began rebuilding it in the new Gothic style of architecture. At the time of Henry's death, the nave of the new church remained unfinished, but was slowly completed over the next 150 years.

In the early sixteenth century, the founder of the Tudor dynasty, Henry VII, added the magnificent Lady Chapel to

Westminster Abbey, 2016. (Author's collection)

the abbey, the highlights of which are his own magnificent tomb that he shares with his wife, Elizabeth of York, and a spectacular fan-vaulted ceiling, with hanging pendants. The chapel was originally decorated with 107 statues of saints, ninety-five of which survive to this day.

In January 1540, the monastery was dissolved, and for the next ten years it functioned as the cathedral church for the diocese of Westminster. The Benedictine monastery was briefly restored under Mary I, only to be refounded as a collegiate church in the reign of Elizabeth I.

In 1745, the iconic western towers were completed.

Henry VIII and Katherine of Aragon:
A Joint Coronation

The abbey has witnessed many momentous occasions, including the coronation of King Henry VIII. Let us briefly step back in time ... On 24 June 1509, Midsummer's Day, Henry VIII and his wife, Katherine of Aragon, walked beneath canopies borne by the barons of the Cinque Ports, from the Palace of Westminster to their coronation at Westminster Abbey. The chronicler Edward Hall recalled that as soon as Katherine and Henry entered the abbey, the striped carpet, which had been laid out for them to walk on, was 'cut and spoiled by the rude and common people', all eager to take home a royal souvenir. The young couple were anointed and crowned by William Warham, the Archbishop of Canterbury, in the presence of prelates of the realm, the nobility and 'a great multitude of commons ...' as recorded by Holinshed in his *Chronicle*. Those present were then asked whether they'd 'receive, obey and take the same most Noble prince for their king?' To which the crowd, with great reverence and love, responded 'yeh, yeh!'

After the formalities, Henry and Katherine processed to Westminster Hall for the coronation banquet, amidst an air of excitement and hope. The virile young king dazzled his people, and many were singing his praises. Thomas More lauded him, 'the everlasting glory of our time ... a king who is worthy not merely to govern a single people but singly to rule the whole world'. William, Baron Mountjoy wrote to the great Dutch Humanist:

> Oh my Erasmus, if you could see how the world here is rejoicing in the possession of so great a prince. Avarice is expelled [from] the land. Liberality scatters riches with a bounteous hand, our king does not desire gold or silver, but virtue, glory, immortality ...

Highlights of the Abbey

You could easily spend a whole day exploring this glorious abbey, and still not see all of its treasures. It's a place to be savoured and explored slowly, at a leisurely pace. Many of the Tudor delights on offer are to be found in the aforementioned Lady Chapel, the beauty of which is guaranteed to leave you speechless. No doubt, once you've managed to tear your gaze away from the spectacular fan-vaulted ceiling, you'll be drawn to the tomb of Henry VII and Elizabeth of York, designed by the Italian sculptor Pietro Torrigiano. Henry and Elizabeth lie in a vault beneath the black marble tomb base, where James VI of Scotland and I of England, is also buried.

Nearby, in the south aisle of the Lady Chapel, James's mother Mary, Queen of Scots, is buried in a splendid marble tomb, which he erected in her memory. Mary was executed at Fotheringhay in 1587, and was originally buried at Peterborough Cathedral, before being moved to the abbey in 1612.

On one side of Mary's great monument, you'll find the tomb of Margaret Beaufort, Countess of Richmond and Derby, and mother of Henry VII, and on the other side, that of Margaret Douglas, Countess of Lennox, the daughter of Archibald Douglas and Margaret Tudor, who was Henry VIII's elder sister.

In the opposite aisle of the chapel (the north aisle), the last of the Tudor monarchs, Elizabeth I, is buried with – or more accurately on top of – her paternal half-sister, Mary I, and beneath a large white marble monument erected by James I. The monument (which James I ensured was not as grand as that of his mother's) bears only the recumbent effigy of Elizabeth I, and resembles portraits of the queen from late in her reign. The Latin inscription on the base, translated, reads: 'Partners both in throne and grave, here rest we two sisters, Elizabeth and Mary, in the hope of the Resurrection'.

One grave easily missed is that of King Edward VI, who was only 9-years-old when he was crowned at the abbey, in February 1547. He is buried close to his grandparents, Henry VII and Elizabeth of York, beneath the original altar of the chapel, in a grave that remained unmarked until the present stone was added in 1966.

As you exit the Lady Chapel, make your way along the south ambulatory to St Edmund's Chapel, where, among others, Frances Brandon, Duchess of Suffolk, is buried. Frances was the daughter of Charles Brandon, Duke of Suffolk, and his third wife, Mary, Henry VIII's younger sister and former queen of France. In 1533, Frances married Henry Grey, Marquess of Dorset, and had, among other issue, three daughters: Jane, Katherine and Mary. Her eldest daughter, Lady Jane Grey, popularly known as 'the nine days' queen, was proclaimed queen after the death of her cousin, Edward VI, however, the country rallied around Mary Tudor, the daughter of Henry VIII and Katherine of Aragon, leading to Lady Jane Grey's overthrow and eventual execution.

There is one more important Tudor tomb to note, another easily missed by visitors to the abbey, that of Henry VIII's fourth wife, Anne of Cleves, who Mary I had buried in a most honoured position, on the south side of the High Altar (where as a sidenote, Anne Neville, wife of Richard III, is also buried in an unmarked grave).

When standing at the foot of the steps, which lead up to the thirteenth-century Cosmati pavement and high altar, Anne of Cleves' monument is on the right, a low stone structure adorned with carvings, which include the initials 'AC' in an oval cartouche, surmounted by a crown, a lion's head, and the emblem of Cleves, an escarbuncle. An inscription was added to the back of the tomb in the 1970s, and is visible from the south transept.

Ironically, Anne, the most overlooked of Henry VIII's queens, is the only one of his wives to be buried in Westminster Abbey. Katherine of Aragon is buried in Peterborough Cathedral, Anne Boleyn's remains are interred in the Chapel of St Peter ad Vincula in the Tower of London, as are those of Catherine Howard, Jane Seymour is buried alongside Henry VIII at

St George's Chapel, Windsor Castle, and Katherine Parr, in St Mary's Church, Sudeley Castle.

Finally, there is one more treasure that is sure to delight the Tudor time traveller, the coronation chair of St Edward the Confessor, which at the time of writing was on display near the great west doors of the abbey. The magnificent oaken chair was made on the orders of King Edward I in 1300–01, to contain the Stone of Scone, and has been used in every coronation ceremony since that of Edward II in 1308. It is quite an amazing thing, to stand just metres away from such a precious artefact, knowing that so many medieval and Tudor kings and queens sat in it to be anointed and crowned. The mystique and grandeur of the coronation ceremony aside, imagining the likes of Henry VIII, Anne Boleyn and Elizabeth I simply sitting in the chair somehow makes them feel more real, more vulnerable, more like us – as if we are somehow connected by the ordinariness of the act.

Leave the coronation chair behind, and make your way along the abbey's central nave towards the high altar. You are now following in the footsteps of all British monarchs on their coronation day. The ceremony itself takes place on the Cosmati pavement in front of the high altar, where the ancient coronation chair, on which the monarch is anointed and crowned, is placed on a carpet, facing the altar.

Do not leave the abbey without seeing the medieval and Tudor artefacts on display in the Abbey Museum, housed in the vaulted undercroft, which include the funeral effigies of Henry VII and Elizabeth I, the Westminster Retable, a thirteenth-century altarpiece, and a ring known as the 'Essex Ring', which Elizabeth I is said to have given to Robert Devereux, 2nd Earl of Essex. Time and weather permitting, take a stroll around the abbey's three main gardens: the Garth, the Little Cloister and the College Garden, which provide a welcome respite from the crowds.

Visitor Information

Westminster Abbey is located in the heart of London, close to the Houses of Parliament and the Jewel Tower (see page 83). I recommend buying your tickets online in advance of your visit and arriving at the abbey at opening time to reduce queuing times. You can also download a free audio guide and pre-purchase abbey guidebooks, ahead of your visit, via their website.

The Cellarium Café & Terrace, housed in the former abbey cellars, serves breakfast, lunch and afternoon tea, and is a lovely place to relax and refuel before beginning or continuing your tour of the abbey.

Those of you unable to visit in person can still explore this great church from the comfort of your home by taking a wonderful online tour available on Westminster Abbey's website.

The closest underground stations are St James's Park and Westminster.

For opening times and other visitor information, visit Westminster Abbey's website at www.westminster-abbey.org

Postcode: SW1P 3PA

Part 4

Museums
& Galleries

Established in 1753, the British Museum is home to well over 6 million artefacts originating from all over the world. Of this extraordinary and vast collection, thousands of items are on public display in more than seventy galleries. The sheer size of the museum can be overwhelming, and while there's no right or wrong way of structuring your visit, I recommend obtaining a map from the Great Court on arrival to help orientate yourself.

Those interested in only seeing items related to medieval and Tudor England should make their way to Level 3, via the North or South stairs, and explore the rooms on the east side, in particular rooms 40 and 46, home to treasures from medieval Europe (1050–1500) and Europe (1400–1800). Also of interest is room 41, the Sir Paul and Lady Ruddock Gallery, where you'll see magnificent objects from an Anglo-Saxon ship burial unearthed in 1939, in Sutton Hoo, Suffolk.

In room 46, keep an eye out for a garter stall-plate made for Sir William Parr, who became a Knight of the Garter in the reign of Henry VIII, was later degraded by Mary I and, finally, restored by Elizabeth I. William was the younger brother of Henry VIII's queen consort, Katherine Parr.

Among the other objects on display is a second garter stall-plate made for another of Henry VIII's one-time brothers-in-law, Sir Edward Seymour, who after Henry's death and during his nephew Edward VI's minority, became Lord Protector of England.

Nearby, is a stunning selection of Tudor jewellery, including rings, pendants and a beautiful girdle prayer book. Look out also for the More Jewels, a collection of five items associated with Thomas More, including a silver seal-die which commemorates More's office as sub-treasurer of England (1521–25).

In a separate cabinet, you'll find a large gold medal from 1545, engraved with the bust of Henry VIII and the inscription, which translated reads, 'Henry VIII, King of England, France, and Ireland, defender of the faith, and under

Christ the supreme head on earth of the Church of England and Ireland'.

Finally, a highlight of the British Museum's Tudor collection is a set of dining silver, made in London between 1581 and 1602 for Sir Christopher Harris (*c.* 1553–1625) and his second wife, Mary Sydenham. Harris worked for Sir Walter Raleigh, whom he helped to redistribute the goods seized during the Anglo-Spanish war, hence why the dining set is sometimes referred to as the 'Armada' service. It comprises of twenty-six serving dishes engraved with the coat-of-arms of the owners and is typical of the dining ware that wealthy Tudors would have owned and used in the late sixteenth century.

Visitor Information

Visiting the British Museum in London is free. The nearest underground stations are Tottenham Court Road and Holborn. Before your visit, I recommend exploring the British Museum's 'Planning your visit' page at www.britishmuseum.org/visiting/planning_your_visit.aspx, for information on museum highlights, audio tours, guided tours, special events and exhibitions, and lunchtime gallery talks, which are free 45-minute presentations given by one of the museum's curators or a guest speaker.

For opening hours and other visitor information go to www.britishmuseum.org

Postcode: WC1B 3DG

Of the nine permanent galleries at the Museum of London, two are of particular interest to the Tudor time traveller: Medieval London (AD 410–1558) and War, Plague & Fire (1550–1660).

The first is home to many wonderful objects associated with everyday life in medieval London, including civilian weaponry; dress accessories, like buckles and brooches; pilgrim and secular badges, and ceramics. Look out for a stunning Saxon brooch decorated with gold and garnets, and pointed medieval shoes known as *poulaine*. Other highlights include a small pewter badge depicting a Tudor rose combined with a pomegranate (the heraldic badge of Katherine of Aragon); an early sixteenth-century altarpiece showing the Angel Gabriel telling the Virgin Mary that she will give birth to a son and name him Jesus; and sixteenth-century rosary beads carved from bone, with a woman's face on one side and a skull on the other. Known as a memento mori, it was designed to remind the owner of her own mortality.

Among the treasures on display in the War, Plague & Fire gallery is a copperplate map of London from about 1558, a beautiful selection of English pottery, including a plate made to commemorate the reign of Elizabeth I, and a wonderful model of the Rose Playhouse, the first Tudor theatre to be built on Bankside. Not long after the theatre's construction in 1587, Christopher Marlowe's *Doctor Faustus*, *The Jew of Malta* and *Tamburlaine the Great* were being performed there, as well as William Shakespeare's *Henry VI Part 1* and *Titus Andronicus*.

As a side note, the Museum of London acquired the Cheapside Hoard in 1912. This remarkable collection of Elizabethan and early Stuart jewellery, uncovered by workmen demolishing a building in Cheapside, is one of the most spectacular finds ever made on British soil. Unfortunately, it is not currently on display, however, some items have been loaned to the British Museum and Victoria and Albert Museum. The Museum of London plans to move to a new site at West

Smithfield (scheduled to open in 2021–22), where they intend to have a purpose-built gallery for the display of the hoard. In the meantime, you can learn more about this dazzling discovery in a wonderful book written by the museum's senior curator of medieval and post-medieval Collections, Hazel Forsyth, entitled *The Cheapside Horde: London's Lost Jewels*. It is available from the museum's gift shop, alongside many other books about the history of London.

Visitor Information

Entry to the Museum of London is free. The nearest underground stations are Barbican and St Paul's, about a 5-minute walk from the museum.

Those of you interested in seeing sections of the Roman wall that once encircled Tudor London, should visit nearby Noble Street and St Alphage Gardens. Consider also joining a tour of the remains of the western gate of London's Roman fort, located in a nearby underground car park. The museum also runs weekend tours of the Billingsgate Roman House and Baths and occasional Roman London walks. Check the Museum of London's website for details.

For opening hours and other visitor information go to www.museumoflondon.org.uk/museum-london

Postcode: EC2Y 5HN

Section of Roman/medieval wall, Noble Street, 2016. (Author's collection)

The Museum of the Order of St John is one of London's lesser-known treasures. It tells the story of the Order of St John, from its beginnings in eleventh-century Jerusalem, where monks established a hospital to care for the many pilgrims who fell sick during their travels to the Holy Land, to its work today in over forty countries around the world.

Not long after this new religious order was established, the men and women who worked there became known as the Hospitallers. After the Crusaders captured Jerusalem in 1099, they continued to care for the sick and the poor, regardless of their race or faith, but the brothers additionally took on a military role and became known as the Knights of the Order of St John of Jerusalem.

By the middle of the twelfth century, a priory in Clerkenwell had been set up as their London headquarters, where it remained until it was dissolved by Henry VIII in 1540, and the priory's lands and wealth seized by the Crown. The order enjoyed a brief revival under the Catholic Mary I, but was again dissolved in the reign of her half-sister, Elizabeth I. After the Dissolution, some of the monastic buildings became the office of the Master of the Revels, where William Shakespeare came to license many of his plays.

Today, the museum occupies two sites in Clerkenwell, London: St John's Gate, which was constructed in 1504 by Prior Thomas Docwra, and once served as the southern entrance to the priory, and the Priory Church of St John, situated just a short walk away. The entrance to the museum's galleries is via an original sixteenth-century chamber of St John's Gate. Visitors are free to browse the fascinating collections that include paintings and illuminated manuscripts, ancient coins, furniture, ceramics and even a bronze canon given to the knights by Henry VIII. However, to access the gatehouse's historic upper-floor rooms and the Priory Church and twelfth-century crypt, you must join a guided tour.

St John's Gate, Clerkenwell, 2016. (Author's collection)

On display in the Chapter Hall is the top illuminated vellum sheet of a contemporary copy of the priory's restoration charter issued by Mary I and Philip II of Spain in 1557. Among the other tour highlights is a magnificent Tudor spiral staircase made of solid blocks of oak, sixteenth-century graffiti carved by a knight, and the church's magnificent Norman crypt, which is home to a sixteenth-century alabaster tomb sculpture of a Spanish knight and an effigy of William Weston,

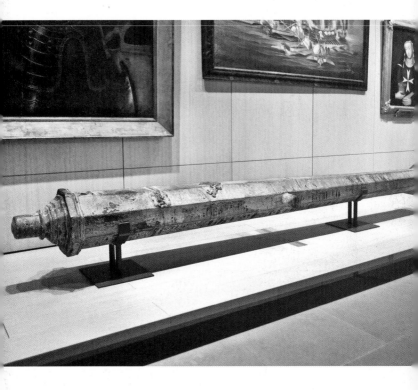

Henry VIII's canon, Museum of the Order of St John, Clerkenwell. This bronze canon was given to the Knights Hospitallers by Henry VIII. (Copyright Peter Eaves, by kind permission of the Museum of the Order of St John)

Tudor stairs, Museum of the Order of St John, Clerkenwell. (Copyright Peter Eaves, by kind permission of the Museum of the Order of St John)

the last prior of the Knights Hospitallers in England. Legend has it that he collapsed and died upon hearing news of the priory's dissolution.

The Church Cloister garden is planted with a selection of herbs that would have been cultivated by the Knights Hospitallers in their medicinal gardens, and is a lovely place to pause and contemplate the rich history of this medieval jewel.

Visitor Information

Entry to the Museum of the Order of St John is free. The nearest underground station is Farringdon, about a 5-minute walk from the museum. Once you exit the station, turn left onto Turnmill Street, and then right onto Benjamin Street, which becomes Albion Place. Continue to the end of the street and turn left onto St John's Lane. St John's Gate will be directly ahead of you.

Guided tours last about 80 minutes and are available on Tuesdays, Fridays and Saturdays at 11 a.m. and 2.30 p.m. As tours are booked on a first come, first served basis, I recommend arriving early, especially at peak times, to avoid disappointment. While the guided tours are free, a suggested donation of £5 per person is most appreciated.

For opening times and visitor information go to www.museumstjohn.org.uk

To watch a virtual tour of the historic buildings visit www.museumstjohn.org.uk/planning-your-visit

Postcode: EC1M 4DA

The National Portrait Gallery in London is home to over 200,000 portraits from the sixteenth century to the present day, including drawings, miniatures, paintings and prints. Of this extraordinary collection, around 1,400 are on public display, including a selection of portraits covering the Tudor and Elizabethan periods, which is second to none.

In the hushed second-floor rooms of the gallery, it's possible to get up close and personal with all the Tudor monarchs and central figures of the day. Room 1 is dedicated to the early Tudors and covers the period from the defeat of Richard III at the Battle of Bosworth in 1485 to the death of Henry VIII in 1547 and the ascension to the throne of Edward and subsequently Mary. Their remarkable story begins aptly with a portrait of the first of the Tudor monarchs, Henry VII, by an unknown artist, painted in October 1505 when the king was 48 years old. It is the earliest painting in the gallery's collection and likely formed part of the unsuccessful marriage negotiations between Henry's court and that of Margaret of Austria's.

Beside the first Tudor king are portraits of his son Henry VIII and his first wife Katherine of Aragon, who came to England from Spain in 1501 as the bride of Henry's older brother, Arthur. The teenager's untimely death, within months of their marriage, left her a widow and paved the way for his younger brother's accession to the throne. While not originally a pair, the portraits of Henry and Katherine are displayed together. They were made in around 1520 when Henry was in his late twenties and Katherine in her mid-thirties. At the time, they'd been married for a little more than a decade and, after at least six recorded pregnancies, had only one surviving child, Princess Mary.

Close to the portrait of Henry VIII is one of Thomas Wolsey, instantly recognisable in his bright red cardinal's robes. For many years, Wolsey was the king's right-hand man and

Archbishop of York, before falling from favour in the late 1520s after failing to secure Henry's divorce from Katherine of Aragon.

Nearby, are two portraits of the woman described by the poet Thomas Wyatt as having 'set our country in a roar' – Anne Boleyn. The first, and most striking of the two, is believed to have been painted in the late sixteenth century and to be based on a now lost contemporary portrait. Anne wears a French hood and her iconic 'B' necklace. The second, painted sometime between 1597 and 1618, appears almost to be a caricature of the first, and is most unflattering.

The stunning full-length portrait of Katherine Parr, for a time thought to be Lady Jane Grey, is attributed to Master John. Take your time savouring the details of Katherine's exquisite gown and jewellery, and get up face to face with the lifelike painting of Thomas Cranmer, painted by the German artist Gerlach Flicke in the final years of Henry's reign.

A late sixteenth- or early seventeenth-century portrait of Mary as queen is also housed in this room. Although not contemporary, it's believed to be based on paintings made during her lifetime by the Flemish artists Hans Eworth and Anthonis Mor. Do not miss the portrait of Mary's younger half-brother, Edward VI, attributed to William Scrots. The 9-year-old heir to the Tudor throne was painted using an intriguing technique called anamorphosis. He appears distorted and stretched, until viewed from the right of the painting.

No doubt the very large and impressive ink and watercolour drawing of Henry VIII by Hans Holbein has already caught your attention. In circa 1536, Henry commissioned a wall painting for Whitehall Palace, and this is the preparatory drawing or cartoon for the left-hand part of that painting. It shows Henry VIII in his famous authoritative pose: legs astride and clenched hands framing his protruding codpiece. He glares at his audience in a defying and aggressive manner. In the background is Henry's father, Henry VII, the founder of the Tudor dynasty, looking nowhere near as intimidating as his son. The other half of the wall painting, for which the preparatory drawing does not survive, showed Henry VIII's mother, Elizabeth of York, and his third wife, Jane Seymour. The wall painting, which Holbein finished in 1537, was destroyed when Whitehall Palace burnt down in 1698.

The adjacent room (Room 2) covers the reign of Elizabeth I, from 1558 until the queen's death in 1603. At the entrance is Elizabeth I's magnificent coronation portrait, depicting the 25-year-old newly crowned queen dressed in dazzling cloth of gold. This room also houses other important portraits of the queen, including one known as the 'Darnley portrait', almost certainly painted from life in around 1575, and the 'Ditchley portrait' by Marcus Gheeraerts the Younger, made for Sir Henry Lee, whose portrait is also displayed here, to commemorate a tournament which Lee organised for Elizabeth in September 1592.

Nearby, are portraits of three of Elizabeth's favourites: her beloved childhood friend and rumoured lover, Robert Dudley, Earl of Leicester, dressed in a striking red suit; a contemporary portrait of Sir Walter Raleigh, painted in 1588, the year the Spanish Armada attacked, and a full-length portrait of Robert Devereux, 2nd Earl of Essex, who eventually fell from the queen's favour and was executed at the Tower of London.

Among other important paintings, is a mid-sixteenth-century portrait of Elizabeth's rival, Mary, Queen of Scots, one of Elizabeth's chief advisors, William Cecil, 1st Baron Burghley, and a full-length portrait of Sir Francis Drake, painted in around 1581, not long after becoming the first Englishman to circumnavigate the globe.

A third room houses a selection of coins and medals, as well as miniatures from the Tudor period. It's also home to special displays, and at the time of writing housed a small exhibit of paintings and miniatures called 'Framing the Face', exploring collars and ruffs in sixteenth- and seventeenth-century dress.

Visitor Information

Entry to the National Portrait Gallery is free. While there is no photography permitted in the galleries, the gift shop stocks a range of postcard reproductions of many of the portraits on display.

The NPG is located in St Martin's Place, London, just a short walk away from the National Gallery, which if you have time to spare is certainly worth a visit. The latter is home to an extensive collection of priceless works of art, including a painting made by Hans Holbein the Younger in 1533, entitled *The Ambassadors*. This elaborate painting depicts Jean de Dinteville, the French ambassador to England and his friend Georges de Selve, bishop of Lavaur, and contains another example of anamorphosis.

The nearest underground stations are Leicester Square and Charing Cross.

For opening times and other visitor information, please visit www.npg.org.uk

Postcode: WC2H 0HE

Tate Britain is home to a collection of British art dating from 1500 to the present day, arranged in a chronological circuit. On the main floor, the gallery labelled 1540 is home to a small but wonderful selection of Tudor portraits including the earliest known full-length portrait of Queen Elizabeth I, painted in c. 1563 and attributed to Steven van der Meulen or Steven van Herwijck.

Nearby, is the earliest picture in the Tate collection, a portrait of an unknown 26-year-old Tudor man painted by John Bettes in 1545, and beside him, a portrait of a man traditionally thought to be William West, 1st Baron de la Warr, standing in a pose reminiscent of Henry VIII in his famous Holbein portrait.

The portrait of a finely dressed young woman is possibly Helena Snakenborg, later Marchioness of Southampton, who came to England in 1565 with Princess Cecelia of Sweden, where she met and later married her first husband, William Parr, Marquess of Northampton. Not long after arriving in England, Helena was appointed as a Maid of Honour to Elizabeth I, whom she loyally served until the queen's death in 1603.

Next to the full-length portrait of Elizabeth, is a portrait of Sir Henry Lee, a favoured Elizabethan courtier, appointed as the Queen's Champion and Master of the Armoury. The painting dates from 1600 when Lee was around 67 years old, his once auburn hair (as seen in his portrait from 1568 on display at the National Portrait Gallery), now completely grey.

In addition to the sixteenth-century portraits is a wonderful early seventeenth-century painting known as *The Cholmondeley Ladies*. The inscription, found in the bottom left corner, reads: 'Two Ladies of the Cholmondeley Family, Who were born the same day, Married the same day, And brought to Bed [gave birth] the same day'. The women are impeccably dressed and depicted sitting beside each other in bed, each cradling their baby wrapped in scarlet fabric.

The other Tudor portraits on display are those of Elizabeth Roydon, Lady Golding, by Hans Eworth, and Elizabeth Cornwallis, Lady Kytson and her husband Sir Thomas Kytson, made by George Gower in 1573.

Visitor Information

Entry to Tate Britain is free. The nearest underground stations are Pimlico and Vauxhall, with Westminster just a short 10 to 15-minute walk away.

For opening times and other visitor information, please go to www.tate.org.uk/visit/tate-britain

Postcode: SW1P 4RG

The Sir John Ritblat Treasures of the British Library Gallery is home to more than 200 fascinating artefacts, including many sixteenth-century treasures. I visited after a long day of sightseeing but was immediately invigorated by the array of fascinating items on display: books, manuscripts, maps, scientific and musical works and personal correspondence, to name but a handful.

Among the highlights are Leonardo da Vinci's notebook, a Gutenberg Bible, Shakespeare's *First Folio*, the Lindisfarne Gospels, and an original copy of Magna Carta. Then there are the letters, a staggeringly beautiful selection of personal correspondence from the Tudor period. Among them, letters penned by Anne Boleyn, Henry VIII, Elizabeth I, Robert Dudley, Mary, Queen of Scots and Thomas Wyatt. All significant moments in Tudor history captured in ink.

This gallery certainly lives up to its name, it is home to treasures of immeasurable beauty and of great global importance, and one can easily spend a couple of hours poring over the various display cabinets. Keep in mind that items are regularly removed from display for conservation reasons, and for use in the library's reading rooms.

Visitor Information

Researchers, academics and students who would like to see a specific item in the library's vast collection of well over 150 million items, the majority of which are held in closed stores, should register for a reader pass. This can be done in person or online at www.bl.uk/help/how-to-get-a-reader-pass

Ensure you allow enough time to visit the library's shop, which houses a wonderful selection of books about medieval and Tudor history, as well as some great bookish gifts for literary lovers, or browse online at www.shop.bl.uk

The Sir John Ritblat Treasures of the British Library Gallery is free to visit and open Monday to Sunday. The nearest underground stations are King's Cross/St Pancras, Euston and Euston Square. For more detailed information on how to reach the British Library and opening times, visit www.bl.uk

Postcode: NW1 2DB

On the south bank of the River Thames, adjacent to Lambeth Palace, stands the Garden Museum, housed in the medieval and Victorian Church of St Mary's, which was deconsecrated in 1972 and saved from demolition by the museum's founder, Rosemary Nicholson.

The museum's collection, comprising of art, photographs, books, diaries, catalogues and historic horticultural tools, explores the story of the British garden from 1600 until the present day. In the courtyard stands a lovely memorial to the Tradescant family, famous seventeenth-century plant collectors and gardeners to King Charles I, who worshipped at St Mary's and were later buried there. Their intricately carved stone tomb is one of the museum's highlights and one of London's most important churchyard monuments.

The Tradescants, though, were not the only notable historical figures to be buried there. Since the first church was built on the site in the eleventh century, an estimated 26,000 burials took place until the churchyard's closure in 1854. Among those buried in the church were several members of one of Tudor England's most powerful families – the Howards, including Agnes Tilney, Dowager Duchess of Norfolk and Elizabeth Boleyn, Countess of Wiltshire, mother of George, Anne and Mary Boleyn.

Elizabeth died on 3 April 1538 at the home of Hugh Faringdon, the Abbot of Reading, which once stood near to Baynard's Castle in London, and was buried on 7 April in a crypt beneath the floor of the Howard Chapel where several of her siblings had already been laid to rest. Elizabeth's paternal half-sister, Lady Katherine Daubeney, served as chief mourner. Sadly, the chapel no longer exists. While some of the Howard monuments were recorded as still extant in the late eighteenth century, no traces of their tombs survive today.

In the early 1970s the church was earmarked for demolition, and so the altar, church bells and pews were removed.

The Garden Museum, Lambeth, 2016. (Author's collection)

Interior of St Mary's Church, Lambeth, c. 1900, where Elizabeth Boleyn was buried in 1538. (Copyright of the Garden Museum)

Thankfully, the ancient church was rescued and repaired by the Tradescant Trust, headed by the aforementioned Mrs Nicholson, and converted into the world's first museum of garden history.

In 2008, it was transformed into a modern museum, complete with exhibition spaces, a café and a shop, and at the time of writing was coming to the end of an extensive redevelopment project.

Visitor Information

The Garden Museum is located on Lambeth Palace Road, on the south bank of the River Thames next to Lambeth Palace. The nearest underground stations are Westminster, Waterloo and Lambeth North. I recommend alighting at Westminster and enjoying the picturesque walk along Millbank and across Lambeth Bridge.

Although the Howard Chapel does not survive, we do know that it once stood north of the chancel, where the café was prior to the latest refurbishment, and roughly where the gift shop will be when the museum is reopened in 2017. Pause for a moment in this area. Where you now stand, a young Catherine Howard, who lived for a time with her step-grandmother at nearby Norfolk House, once sat in prayer. What did she hope for her life in those days before she was catapulted to the dizzying heights of royalty?

Spare a thought also for Elizabeth Boleyn, who died in 1538 a broken woman, after the execution of her children Anne and George Boleyn. Her mortal remains lie buried somewhere beneath the floor, alongside many other members of her family.

While visiting the museum, take note of the Novotel London Waterloo Hotel, virtually opposite St Mary's

Interior of St Mary's Church, Lambeth, *c.* 1977, before its restoration and conversion into a museum of garden history. (Copyright of the Garden Musuem)

Church, as this roughly marks the site of Norfolk House, the grand London residence of the Dukes of Norfolk, where Catherine Howard spent years in the care of her step-grandmother, Agnes Tilney, Dowager Duchess of Norfolk, before her marriage to Henry VIII. It's during this time that Catherine is said to have become romantically involved with Henry Manox and Francis Dereham.

The house once boasted extensive gardens and orchards, the remains of which can be seen in the nearby Old Paradise Gardens. On exiting the museum, cross the road and walk up Lambeth High Street, where you'll soon see the entrance to the gardens.

At the time of writing, the Garden Museum was closed to the public and expected to reopen in early 2017. Please check their website for details: www.gardenmuseum.org.uk

Postcode: SE1 7LB

THE NATIONAL ARCHIVES

Set in beautiful grounds just a short walk from the River Thames and Kew Gardens, the National Archives is home to millions of historical documents, known as records, covering more than 1,000 years of history. Among the Tudor highlights is a letter written by Catherine Howard to Thomas Culpeper (1541); a great seal of Elizabeth I used during the second half of her reign; portraits of Elizabeth I from crown plea rolls; a letter written by Sir Francis Drake, vice-admiral of the English fleet, to Sir Francis Walsingham, principal secretary to Elizabeth I, after the Battle of Gravelines (1588); and the will of the world's most famous playwright, William Shakespeare, dated 25 March 1616.

While not on permanent display, visitors can request to view original documents in the archives' reading rooms. There is also a bookshop and restaurant on site, and a museum called the Keeper's Gallery, which features highlights from the National Archives, and houses temporary document displays. At the time of writing, Shakespeare's will was on public display to mark the 400th anniversary of his death.

The National Archives also offers a range of events and talks that, while usually free of charge, still need to be pre-booked. Keep an eye on their website for events that might coincide with your planned visit.

Visitor Information

Kew Gardens Station is less than a kilometre away from the National Archives. While you're in the area, you might also like to visit the remains of Richmond Palace, a favoured Tudor residence, where Henry VII and Elizabeth I died in 1509 and 1603, respectively. To see all that survives above ground – the main gateway and part of the outer range, once the palace wardrobe – make your way from Kew Gardens Station to Richmond Station, and then to the west side of Richmond Green. Also of interest to the Tudor time traveller is Richmond Park, the largest of London's royal parks, and one that boasts royal connections going back as far as the thirteenth century.

King Henry's Mound, the highest point in the park, was named so because it was traditionally thought to be where Henry VIII heard the Tower of London's canon fire on the morning of 19 May 1536, announcing the execution of his second wife, Anne Boleyn. An interesting but apocryphal story, as most modern historians agree that Henry received news of Anne's death at Whitehall Palace. Nevertheless, it's worth visiting for the outstanding views alone. For park opening times and other visitor information go to www.royalparks.org.uk/parks/richmond-park

For information on how to reach the National Archives, upcoming events and opening times, visit www.nationalarchives.gov.uk

Postcode: TW9 4DU

The Victoria and Albert Museum in London, also known as the V&A, is the world's leading museum of art and design, its vast collection unrivalled in its richness and diversity. It's home to some extraordinary objects from around the world, including furniture, fashion, jewellery, sculptures, textiles, ceramics and paintings. Each year, several million people walk through its doors to see the 60,000 or so items on permanent display, including a remarkable collection of treasures from the medieval and Renaissance period.

With 146 rooms arranged across six levels, I recommend obtaining a map on arrival and locating the Medieval & Renaissance and Britain (1500–1760) Galleries on Level 0, 1 and 2, where you'll find many tantalising Tudor treasures.

A definite standout, and one of the largest objects in the museum, is the timber façade of a house constructed in 1600 on Bishopsgate Street for Sir Paul Pindar, a wealthy English merchant and diplomat. Most timber-framed houses in London were destroyed in the Great Fire of 1666 and so this is a rare and wonderful relic.

Among the many other highlights is a fountain attributed to the Florentine sculptor Benedetto da Rovezzano, which once stood in the great court of Cowdray House in Sussex, largely destroyed by fire in 1793, and a beautiful walnut writing box, made in about 1525, and decorated with the royal arms and badges of Henry VIII and Katherine of Aragon. Nearby, is a portrait of Henry VIII and a portrait bust of his father, Henry VII, made by the Florentine sculptor Pietro Torrigiani between 1509 and 1511. The bust is based on Henry VII's death mask and so is presumably a very good likeness of the first Tudor monarch.

Keep an eye out for fragments of a terracotta relief that once decorated Suffolk Place in Southwark, the London home of Charles Brandon, Duke of Suffolk; a miniature portrait of Anne of Cleves painted by Hans Holbein in 1539 and a miniature whistle pendant, shaped like a pistol, which houses cosmetic tools in the stock, and according to legend, was the first of many gifts given by Henry VIII to Anne Boleyn.

Further on in the gallery is a tapestry that was made in around 1585, which bears the arms of Robert Dudley, Earl of Leicester, who is believed to have commissioned it for his London home, Leicester House, and an enormous bed, known as the Great Bed of Ware, that dates back to at least 1596. This is one of the museum's most popular objects on account of its great size. The four-poster bed is over 3m wide and can reputedly accommodate eight people. It was probably made in the 1590s for an Inn at Ware in Hertfordshire, and quickly became famous. Shakespeare referred to it in his play *Twelfth Night*, obviously confident that his readers would understand the reference.

Do not miss Nicholas Hilliard's miniature portraits of Elizabeth I, Mary, Queen of Scots, Robert Dudley and Sir Christopher Hatton, as well as a portrait of Mary, Queen of Scots, aged around 17, painted by a follower of François Clouet. Also associated with the Scottish queen are a number of panels, which Mary is said to have embroidered with Elizabeth Talbot, Countess of Shrewsbury, better known as Bess of Hardwick, during her imprisonment.

Finally, look out for the Hunsdon Jewels, which, according to tradition, Elizabeth I gave to her cousin, Henry Carey, 1st Baron Hunsdon, the son of Elizabeth's maternal aunt, Mary Boleyn, and a set of virginals decorated with the royal coat of arms and Anne Boleyn's falcon badge. The late Professor Eric Ives believed it was possible that the virginals may have originally belonged to Anne before her daughter, Elizabeth I, acquired them.

To wander through the many galleries and stand just a few inches away from objects that the Tudors would have seen, held and worn, is a stirring experience, and one that greatly strengthens our connection with them. They cease to be just names in history books and instead become very real – very human.

Visitor Information

Admission to the Victoria and Albert Museum is free. The nearest underground station is South Kensington. At the information desk you'll find information on the latest exhibitions, talks and tours, including free daily introductory tours of the Medieval & Renaissance and Britain Galleries.

For opening hours and other visitor information go to www.vam.ac.uk

Postcode: SW7 2RL

LIST OF ILLUSTRATIONS

The map of Tudor London and the surrounding area was created by Kathryn Holeman from KSH Creative.

1. Tyburn Tree (Gallows) Plaque, London. (Author's collection)
2. The Old Royal Naval College, Greenwich, London. (Author's collection)
3. A nineteenth-century reconstruction of the City of London and its Environs in Tudor times by H.W. Brewer. (Author's collection)
4. A reconstruction of Tudor Cheapside. (Author's collection)
5. Temple Bar, London. (Author's collection)
6. A nineteenth-century reconstruction of the City of London and its Environs in Tudor times by H.W. Brewer. (Author's collection)
7. A nineteenth-century reconstruction of the City of London and its Environs in Tudor times by H.W. Brewer. (Author's collection)
8. The Great Hall at Eltham Palace. (Copyright Sarah Morris)
9. The (West) Tudor Courtyard, Fulham Palace, London. (Author's collection, by permission of Fulham Palace)
10. All Saint's Church, Fulham, London. (Author's collection)
11. Guildhall, London. (Author's collection)
12. Interior of the Great Hall, Guildhall, London. (Author's collection, by kind permission of the City of London Corporation)
13. Early twentieth-century painting of Hampton Court Palace, Surrey. (Author's collection)
14. Hampton Court Palace, Surrey. (Author's collection)
15. View of the north of Hampton Court Palace made by Anton van den Wyngaerde in 1558. (By kind permission of the Stationery Office)
16. View of the south of Hampton Court Palace made by Anton van den Wyngaerde in 1558. (By kind permission of the Stationery Office)

17. The banqueting houses, Hampton Court Palace, from a drawing by Anton van den Wyngaerde made in 1558. (By kind permission of the Stationery Office)
18. The Jewel Tower, Westminster, London. (Author's collection)
19. Tudor Westminster, viewed from the east. (Author's collection)
20. Victoria Tower, Palace of Westminster, London. (Author's collection)
21. Morton's Tower, Lambeth Palace, Westminster, London. (Author's collection)
22. The Gateway, Lincoln's Inn, by E.W. Haslehust. (Image copyright Bruce Hunt, maps.thehunthouse.com)
23. Staple Inn, London. (Author's collection)
24. Sutton House, Hackney, London. (Author's collection)
25. The Tower of London viewed from the south. (Author's collection)
26. Plan of the Tower of London in 1597, by Haiward and Gascoyne. (Author's collection)
27. Reconstruction of the Tower of London, as it would have appeared in the sixteenth century. (Author's collection)
28. Early twentieth-century photo of the interior of the Chapel of St Peter ad Vincula, Tower of London. (Author's collection)
29. The Byward Tower, Tower of London. (Author's collection)
30. Site of the scaffold on Tower Hill, c. 1900. (Author's collection)
31. Site of the scaffold on Tower Hill, London. (Author's collection)
32. Old St Paul's Cathedral. (Author's collection)
33. King Henry VIII from Foxe's *Book of Martyrs* 1563. (By kind permission of the Stationery Office)
34. All Hallows by the Tower, London. (Author's collection)
35. Chelsea Old Church, Chelsea. (Author's collection)
36. Statue of Thomas More, Chelsea Old Church. (Author's collection)
37. Christchurch Greyfriars Church Garden, London. (Author's collection)
38. Southwark Cathedral, Southwark, London. (Author's collection)
39. Ruins of Winchester Palace, Southwark, London. (Author's collection)
40. St Bartholomew the Great, West Smithfield, London. (Author's collection)

FURTHER READING

Bergenroth, G.A., ed., *Calendar of State Papers, Spain, Volume 1, 1485–1509* (London: 1862)

Bray, W., ed., *The Diary of John Evelyn* (New York & London: George G. Harrop, 1960)

Brears, P., *All the King's Cooks: The Tudor Kitchens of King Henry VIII at Hampton Court Palace* (London: Souvenir Press, 2011)

Byrne, C., *Katherine Howard: A New History* (MadeGlobal Publishing, 2014)

Chandler, J., *John Leland's Itinerary: Travels in Tudor England* (Stroud: Sutton Publishing, 1993)

Clifford, A., ed., *The State Papers and Letters of Sir Ralph Sadler* (London: T. Cadell and W. Davies, William Miller and John Murray, 1809)

Colvin, H.M., *The History of the King's Works: Volume IV 1485–1660 (Part II)* (London: Her Majesty's Stationery Office, 1982)

Crankshaw, D.J., 'The Tudor Privy Council, *c.* 1540–1603', *State Papers Online, 1509–1714* (Reading: Cengage Learning EMEA Ltd, 2009)

Davies, G.S., *Charterhouse in London: Monastery, Mansion, Hospital, School* (London: J. Murray, 1921)

De Lisle, L., *Tudor: The Family Story* (London: Chatto & Windus, 2013)

Edelen, G., ed., *The Description of England. The Classic Contemporary Account of Tudor Social Life by William Harrison* (Washington and New York: The Folger Shakespeare Library & Dover Publications, 1994)

Emery, A., *Greater Medieval Houses of England and Wales: 1300–1500, Volume III, Southern England* (Cambridge: Cambridge University Press 2006)

Falcus, C., ed., *The Private Lives of the Tudor Monarchs* (London: The Folio Society, 1974)

Fox, J., *Sister Queens: Katherine of Aragon and Juana, Queen of Castile* (London: Phoenix, 2011)

Gairdner, J., ed., *Letters and Papers: Foreign and Domestic, Henry VIII, Volume 5* (1880)

Gairdner, J., ed., *Letters and Papers: Foreign and Domestic, Henry VIII, Volume 6* (1882)

Gairdner, J., ed., *Letters and Papers: Foreign and Domestic, Henry VIII, Volume 7* (1883)

Gairdner, J., ed., *Letters and Papers: Foreign and Domestic, Henry VIII, Volume 8* (1885)

Gairdner, J., ed., *Letters and Papers: Foreign and Domestic, Henry VIII, Volume 9* (1886)

Gairdner, J., ed., *Letters and Papers: Foreign and Domestic, Henry VIII, Volume 10* (1887)

Goodman, R., *How to be a Tudor: A Dawn-to-Dusk Guide to Everyday Life* (London: Viking, 2015)

Groos, G.W., ed., *The Diary of Baron Waldstein: A Traveller in Elizabethan England* (London: Thames and Hudson, 1981)

Hayward, M., *Dress at the Court of King Henry VIII* (Leeds: Maney Publishing, 2007)

Historic Towns Trust, *A Map of Tudor London: 1520* (London: Old House Books, 2008)

Hunt, A., *The Drama of Coronation: Medieval Ceremony in Early Modern England* (Cambridge: Cambridge University Press, 2008)

Hunt, A., & Whitelock, A., eds, *Tudor Queenship: The Reigns of Mary and Elizabeth* (New York: Palgrave Macmillan, 2010)

Inwood, S., *Historic London: An Explorer's Companion* (London: Pan Macmillan, 2008)

Ives, E., *The Life and Death of Anne Boleyn* (Oxford: Blackwell Publishing, 2004)

Jennings, A., *Tudor and Stuart Gardens* (Swindon: English Heritage, 2005)

Kettler, S.V., & Trimble, C., *The Amateur Historian's Guide to Medieval & Tudor London* (Virginia: Capital Books, 2001)

Kingsford, C.L., ed., *A Survey of London by John Stow* (Oxford: Clarendon, 1908)

Kipling, G., ed. *The Receyt of the Ladie Kateryne* (Oxford: Oxford University Press, 1990)

Licence, A., *In Bed with the Tudors* (Stroud: Amberley Publishing, 2012)

Lipscomb, S., *A Visitor's Companion to Tudor England* (London: Ebury Press, 2012)

Moore, J., & Nero, P., *Ye Olde Good Inn Guide: A Tudor Traveller's Guide to the Nation's Finest Taverns* (Stroud: The History Press, 2013)

Morris, S., & Grueninger, N., *In the Footsteps of Anne Boleyn* (Stroud: Amberley Publishing, 2013)

Morris, S., & Grueninger, N., *In the Footsteps of the Six Wives of Henry VIII* (Stroud: Amberley Publishing, 2016)

Mortimer, I., *The Time Traveller's Guide to Elizabethan England* (London: The Bodley Head, 2012)

Mount, T., *Everyday Life in Medieval London: From the Anglo-Saxons to the Tudors* (Stroud: Amberley Publishing, 2014)

Nichols, J.G., ed., *Chronicle of the Greyfriars of London* (London: The Camden Society, 1851)

Nichols, J., *The Progresses and Public Processions of Queen Elizabeth* (London: Jon Nichols & Sons, 1823)

Norton, E., *Anne of Cleves: Henry VIII's Discarded Bride* (Stroud: Amberley Publishing, 2010)

Penn, T., *Winter King: The Dawn of Tudor England* (London: Penguin Books, 2012)

Pevsner, N., & Cherry, B., *The Buildings of England – London 4: North* (New Haven and London: Yale University Press, 2002)

Picard, L., *Elizabeth's London: Everyday Life in Elizabethan London* (New York: St Martin's Griffin, 2003)

Plowden, A., *Tudor Women: Queen & Commoners* (Stroud: The History Press, 2010)

Quennell, P., ed., *Life in Tudor England by Penry Williams* (London: William Clowes & Sons, 1964)

Rex, R., *The Tudors*, (Stroud: Amberley Publishing, 2011)

Ridgway, C., *On This Day in Tudor History* (MadeGlobal Publishing, 2012)

Roberts, H., & Godfrey, W., eds, *Survey of London: Volume 23, Lambeth* (London: London County Council, 1951)

Robertson, A.G., *Discovering London: Tudor London* (London: Macdonald & Co., 1968)

Samman, N., *The Henrician Court During Cardinal Wolsey's Ascendancy: c. 1514–1529* (PhD thesis, University of Wales, 1988)

Sim, A., *Food and Feast in Tudor England* (Stroud: Sutton Publishing Limited, 1997)

Sim, A., *Pleasures & Pastimes in Tudor England* (Stroud: The History Press, 2009)

Sim, A., *The Tudor Housewife* (Stroud: The History Press, 2010)

Starkey, D., ed., *Henry VIII: A European Court in England* (New York: Cross River Press, 1991)

Starkey, D., ed., *Rivals in Power: Lives and Letters of the Great Tudor Dynasties* (London: Macmillan, 1990)

Starkey, D., ed., *The Inventory of Henry VIII: The Transcript*, Vols 1 and 2 (London: Society of Antiquaries & Harvey Miller, 1998)

Starkey, D., *Elizabeth: The Struggle for the Throne* (New York: Harper Collins, 2001)

Starkey, D., *Henry: Virtuous Prince* (London: Harper Press, 2008)

Sylvester, R., ed., *The Life and Death of Cardinal Wolsey by George Cavendish* (London: Oxford University Press, 1959)

Tallis, N., *Crown of Blood: The Deadly Inheritance of Lady Jane Grey* (New York: Pegasus Books, 2016)

Thomas, D., *A Visitor's Guide to Shakespeare's London* (Barnsley: Pen & Sword Books, 2016)

Thornbury, W., & Walford, E., eds, *Old and New London: Volume 1–6* (London: Cassell, Petter & Galpin, 1878)

Thurley, S., *The Royal Palaces of Tudor England* (London: Yale University Press, 1993)

Thurley, S., *Hampton Court: A Social and Architectural History* (London: Yale University Press, 2003)

Tremlett, G., *Catherine of Aragon: Henry's Spanish Queen* (London: Faber and Faber, 2010)

Weir, A., *Henry VIII: King & Court* (London: Vintage Books, 2008)

Williams, C., ed., *Thomas Platters Travels in England 1599* (London: Jonathan Cape, 1937)

Wriothesley, C., *A Chronicle during the Reign of the Tudors* (London: Longmans, Green etc., 1838)

GUIDEBOOKS

All Hallows by the Tower

Charterhouse

Eltham Palace

Fulham Palace and Gardens: A Brief History

Hampton Court Palace

Lambeth Palace

Museum of the Order of St John

Saint Bartholomew the Great

Southwark Cathedral

St Dunstan-in-the-West

St Etheldreda's, Ely Place
Sutton House
The Jewel Tower
The Tower of London

INTERNET RESOURCES

John Strype's *A Survey of the Cities of London and Westminster*
www.hrionline.ac.uk/strype

The Diary of Samuel Pepys
www.pepysdiary.com

AUTHOR CONTACT INFORMATION

To get in touch with Natalie Grueninger please visit:

www.onthetudortrail.com
www.nataliegrueninger.com

Facebook.com/
OntheTudorTrailRetracingthestepsofAnneBoleyn
Facebook.com/nataliegrueningerauthor
Twitter: @OntheTudorTrail
Instagram: themosthappy78

INDEX